John R. Sweney

Our Praise in Song

A collection of hymns and sacred melodies, adapted for use by Sunday schools,

Endeavor societies, Epworth leagues, evangelists

John R. Sweney

Our Praise in Song

A collection of hymns and sacred melodies, adapted for use by Sunday schools, Endeavor societies, Epworth leagues, evangelists

ISBN/EAN: 9783337083977

Printed in Europe, USA, Canada, Australia, Japan

Cover: Foto ©Lupo / pixelio.de

More available books at **www.hansebooks.com**

Our PRAISE in SONG:

A COLLECTION OF

HYMNS AND SACRED MELODIES,

ADAPTED FOR USE BY

Sunday Schools, Endeavor Societies,
Epworth Leagues, Evangelists,
Pastors, Choristers, etc.

EDITORS:

**JNO. R. SWENEY, W. J. KIRKPATRICK
AND H. L. GILMOUR.**

PHILADELPHIA:
John J. Hood,
1024 Arch Street.

COPYRIGHT, 1893, BY JOHN J. HOOD.

FROM the beginning praise
   Has best expressed itself in holy song,
   By the lone heart or the exultant throng;—
So childhood, youth, and hoary age prolong
     Gladness in jubal lays.
On mountain heights, or by the rolling sea,
Let every heart break forth in hallowed melody.

II.

   Here heaven and earth unite,—
Song fell from heaven when Christ the Lord was born,
Song cheers the heart when earth is all forlorn;
Then, sing at night, and in the early morn;—
     Sing in supreme delight;
Sing praise to God; go, praise him, and adore,
Till all shall meet above, then praise forevermore.

Ocean Grove, N. J., May, 1893.   —E. H. STOKES.

COPYRIGHT NOTICE.

To PRINT, for sale or otherwise, any copyright hymn of this collection, unless written permission shall have been obtained, is an infringement of copyright.

THE PUBLISHER.

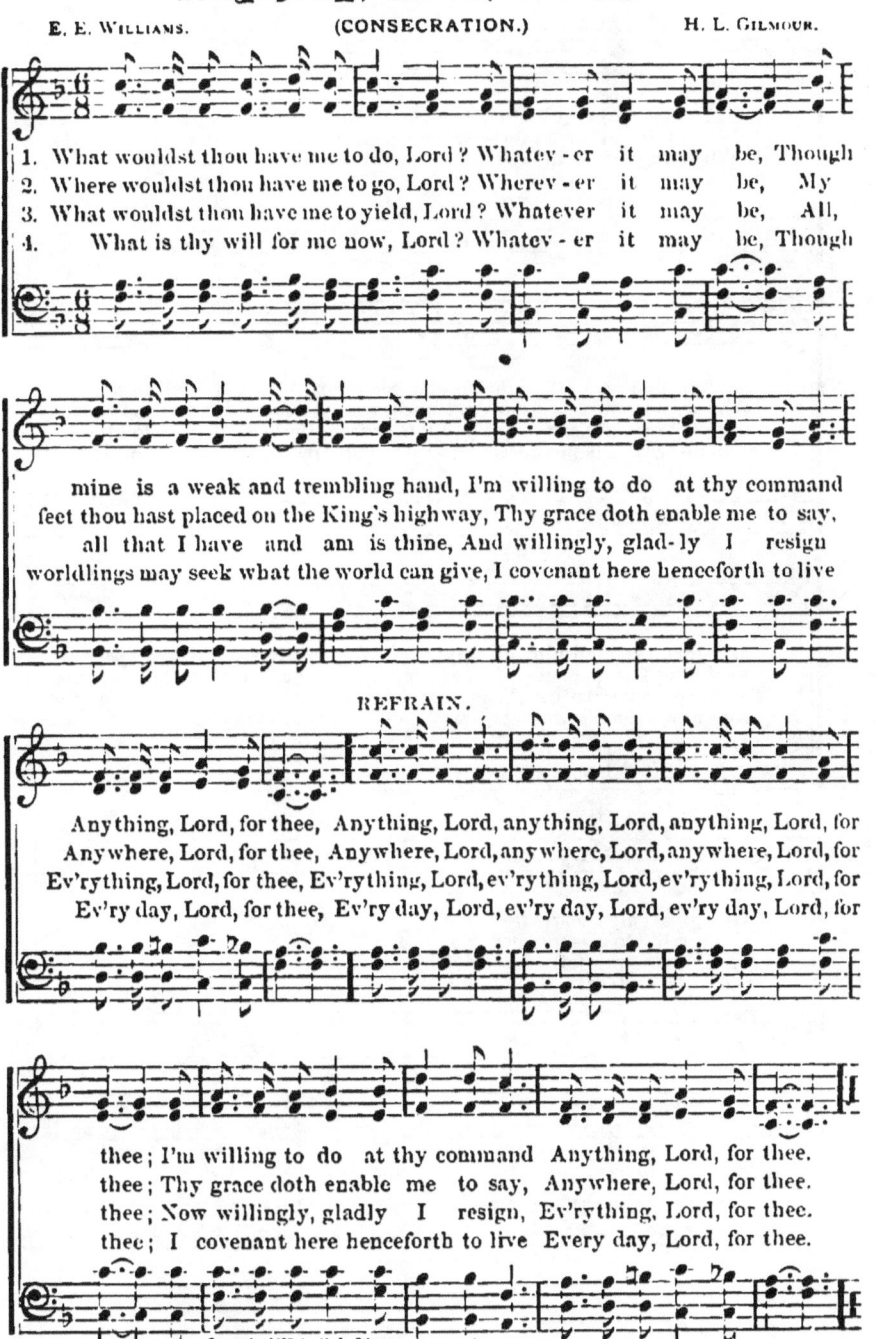

He is My Refuge.

F. A. Blackmer.

1. I always go to Jesus When troubled or distressed, I always find a refuge Upon his loving breast; I tell him all my trials, I tell him all my grief, And while my lips are speaking He gives my heart relief.

2. When full of dread foreboding, And flowing o'er with tears, He calms away my sorrow And hushes all my fears; He comprehends my weakness, The peril I am in, And he supplies the armor I need to conquer sin.

3. When those are cold and faithless Who once were fond and true, With careless hearts forsaking The old friends for the new, I turn to him whose friendship Knows neither change nor end; I always find in Jesus A never-failing friend.

4. I always go to Jesus, No matter when or where I seek his gracious presence, I'm sure to find him there. In times of joy or sorrow, Whate'er my need may be, I always go to Jesus, And Jesus comes to me.

REFRAIN.

He is my refuge, He is my refuge, He is my refuge, My never-failing friend.

Copyright, 1893, by John J. Hood.

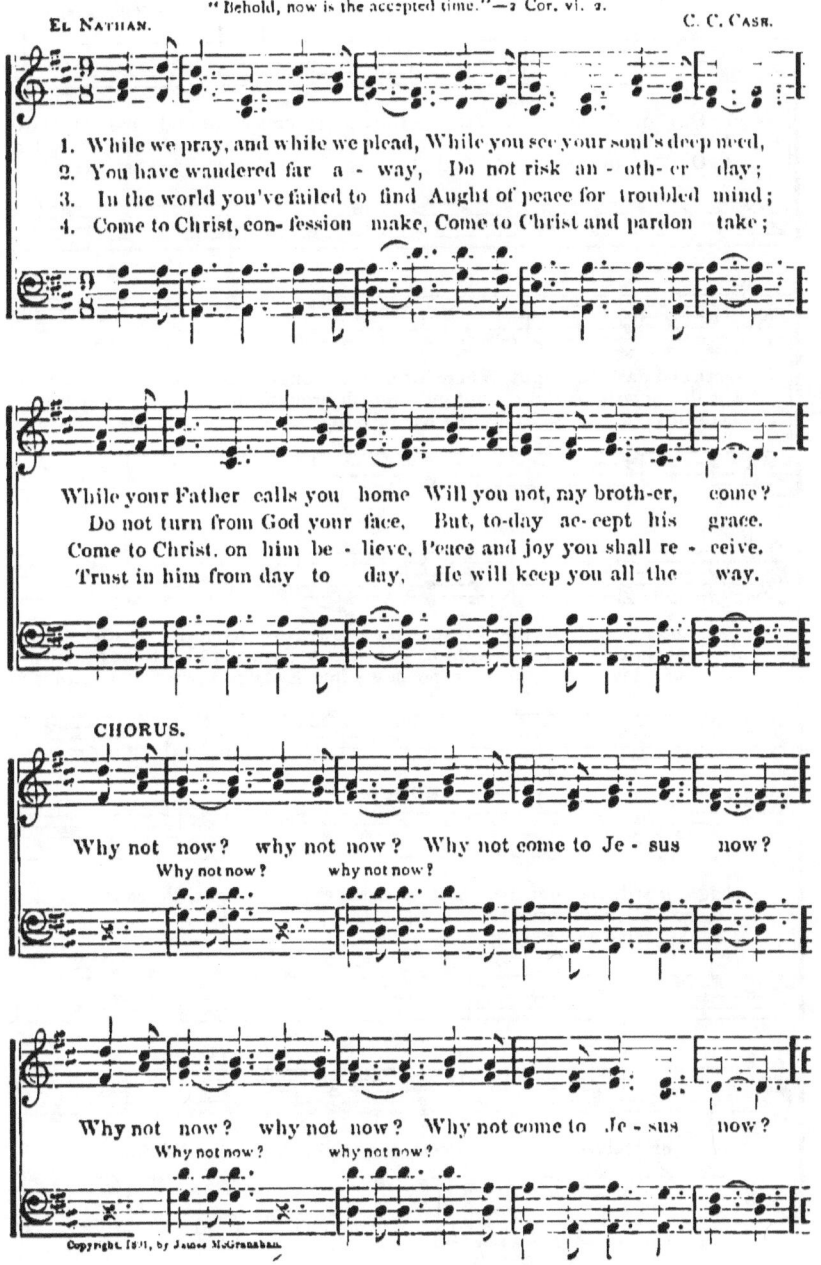

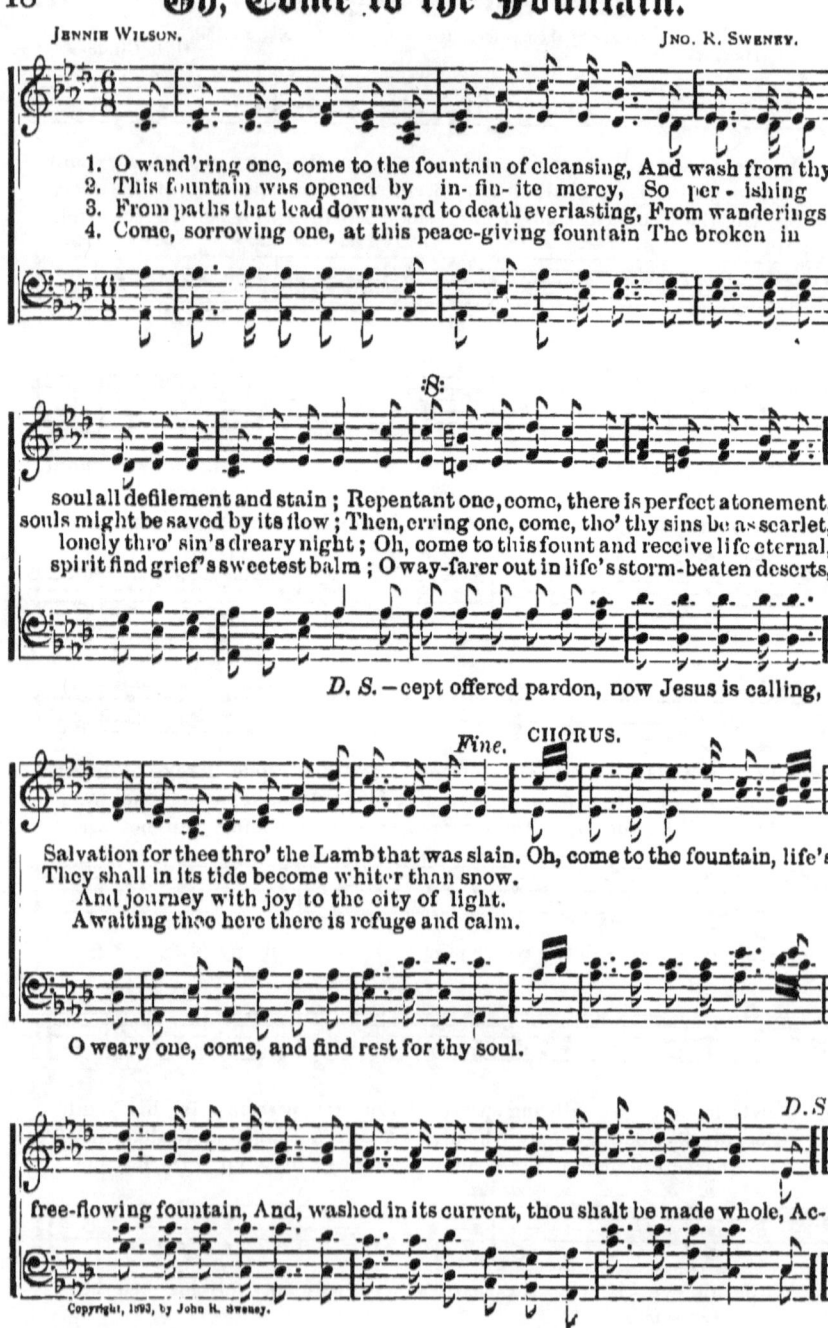

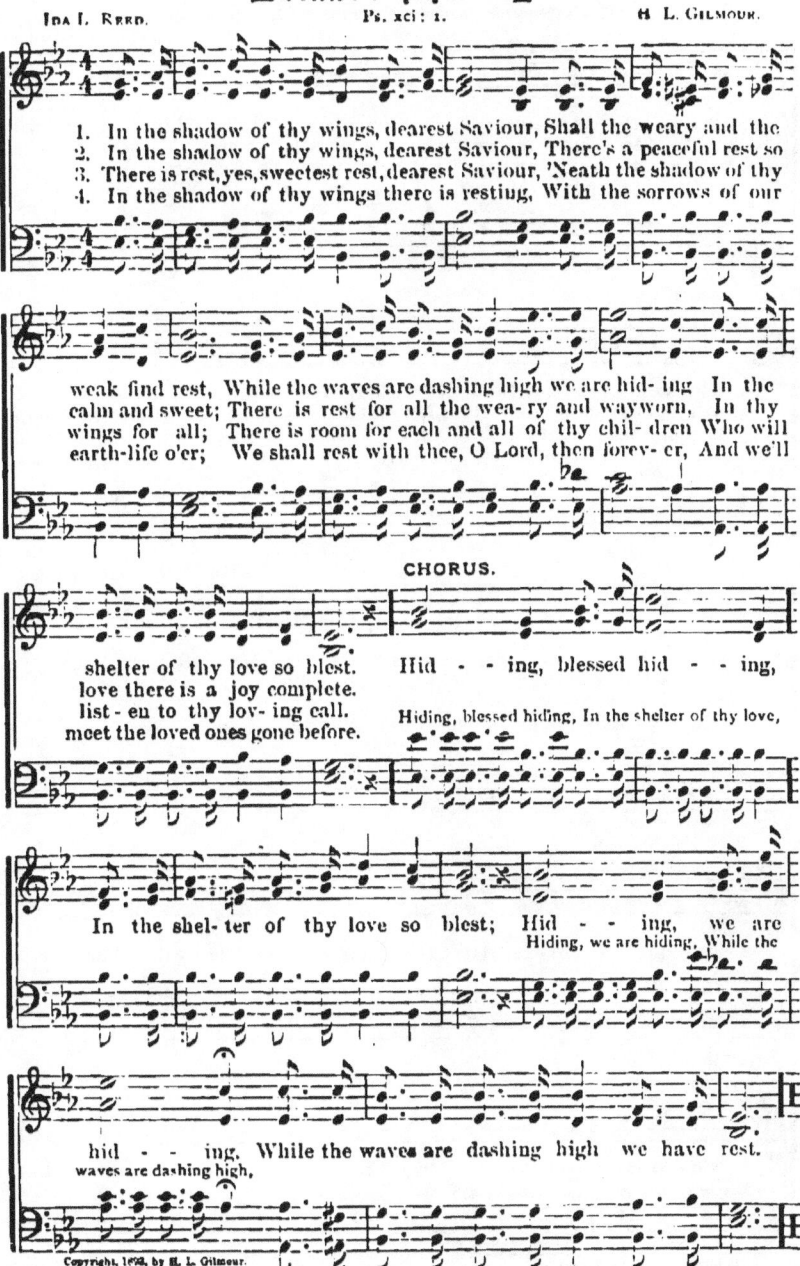

20. On to Victory.

JENNIE WILSON. "This is the victory that overcometh the world." 1 John v: 4. JNO. R. SWENEY.

1. "On to vic-to-ry" shall our mot-to be, While we march as soldiers of Christ our Lord; Ne'er shall come defeat when the foe we meet, If for bat-tle or-ders we take God's word.
2. "On to vic-to-ry," for on Cal-va-ry Je-sus conquered death that our souls might live; Let us trust his name, and his promise claim, In the Christian warfare he'll triumph give.
3. "On to vic-to-ry," till the world is free From the cru-el bondage and blight of sin; Onward, onward press, gaining new success, Stars to shine for-ev-er thro' Je-sus win.
4. "On to vic-to-ry," till those heights we see Where the an-gel arm-ies of Jesus stand, Then with joyous song we shall join the throng, Singing happy praise in the glo-ry-land.

CHORUS.

"On to vic-to-ry, on to vic-to-ry," Hear the ringing bat-tle call, "On to vic-to-ry, on to vic-to-ry," Earth shall crown him Lord of all.

Copyright, 1895, by Jno. R. Sweney.

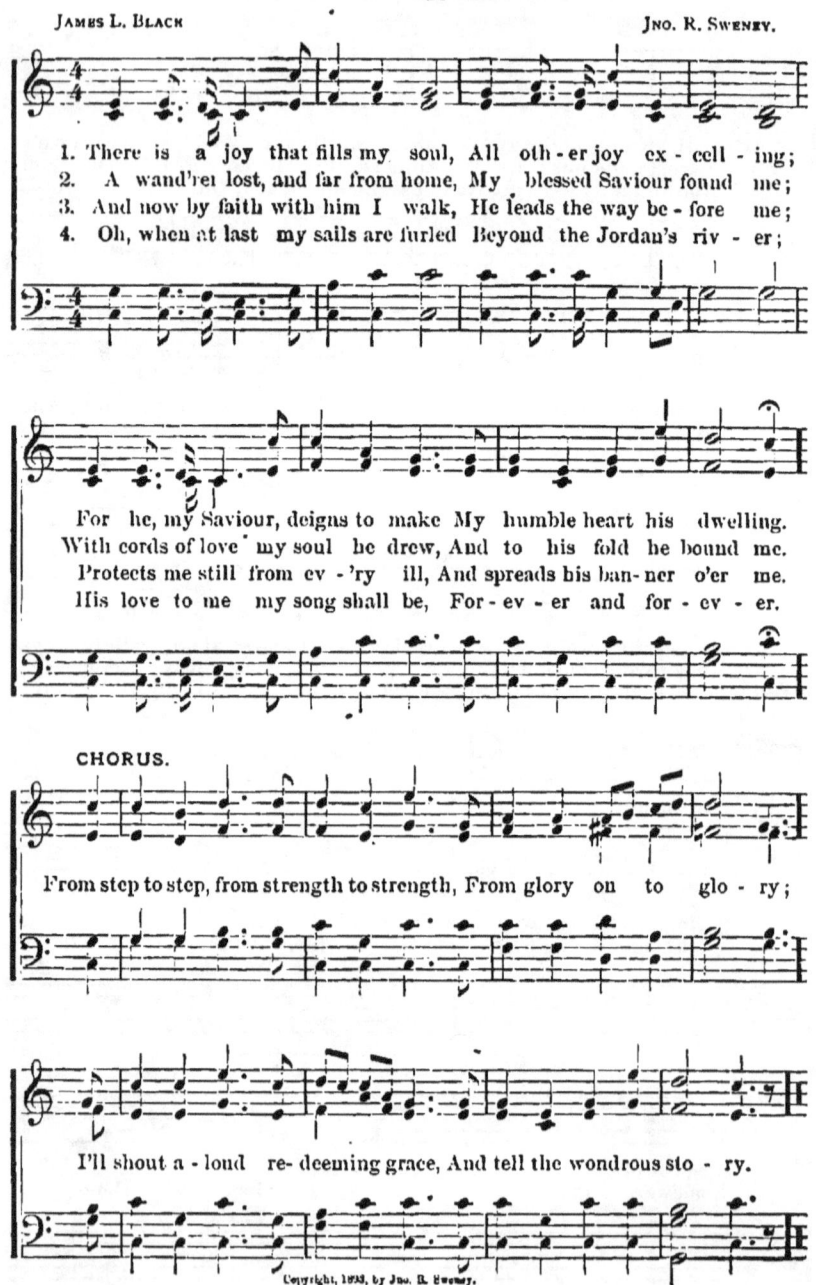

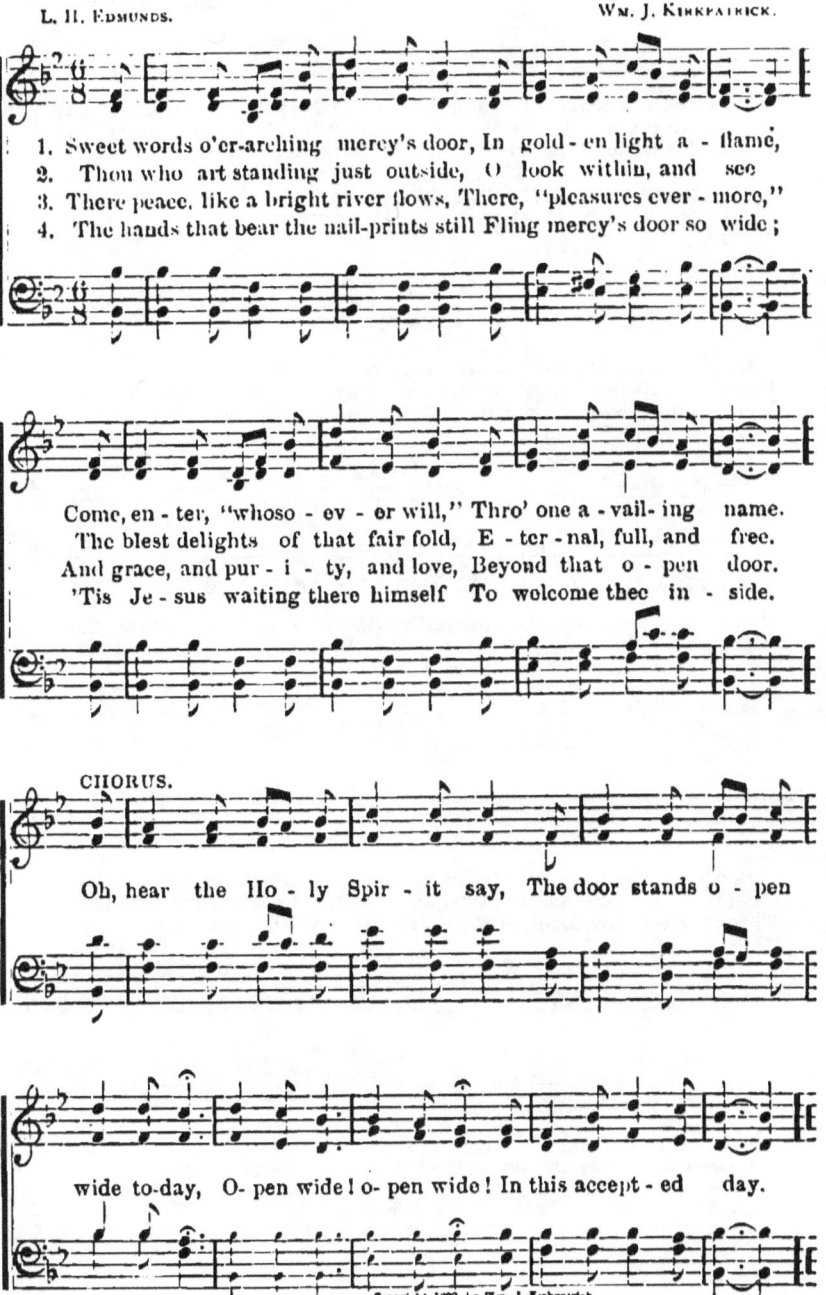

I'll Sing my Dear Redeemer's Praise. 27

L. H. Edmunds.
Wm. J. Kirkpatrick.

1. I'll sing my dear Redeemer's praise, "Rejoice with me" to-day, For Jesus smiled upon my soul, And took my sins away.
2. I heard a voice that filled the night With music pure and sweet, I felt a touch that healed my wounds, And drew me to his feet.
3. He led me to his pastures green, Where streams of mercy flow, And taught my heart the happy song None but his ransomed know.
4. Oh, sweeter yet that song shall rise, Until his face I see, And tell the wond'ring angels 'round, That Jesus died for me.

CHORUS.

Oh, glory to his name And his wondrous love proclaim, I'll shout his praise on high; I'll sing redeeming love To the shining hosts a-bove, And behold his face in glo-ry by and by.

Copyright, 1886, by Wm. J. Kirkpatrick.

Throw Out the Life-Line.

(May be sung as a Solo and Chorus.)

Rev. E. S. Ufford. E. S. U. Arr. by Geo. C. Stebbins.

1. Throw out the life-line a-cross the dark wave, There is a brother whom some one should save; Somebod-y's brother! oh, who then, will dare To throw out the life-line, his per-il to share?
2. Throw out the life-line with hand quick and strong: Why do you tarry, why lin-ger so long? See! he is sinking, oh, hast-en to day—And out with the life-boat! a-way, then, a-way
3. Throw out the life-line to danger-fraught men, Sinking in anguish where you've nev-er been: Winds of temptation and bil-lows of woe Will soon hurl them out where the dark waters flow.
4. Soon will the season of res-cue be o'er, Soon will they drift to e-ter-ni-ty's shore, Haste then, my brother, no time for de-lay, But throw out the life-line, and save them to-day.

CHORUS.

Throw out the life-line! Throw out the life-line! Some one is drifting a-way; Throw out the life-line! Throw out the life-line! Some one is sinking to-day.

Copyright, 1890, by The Biglow & Main Co. Used by permission.

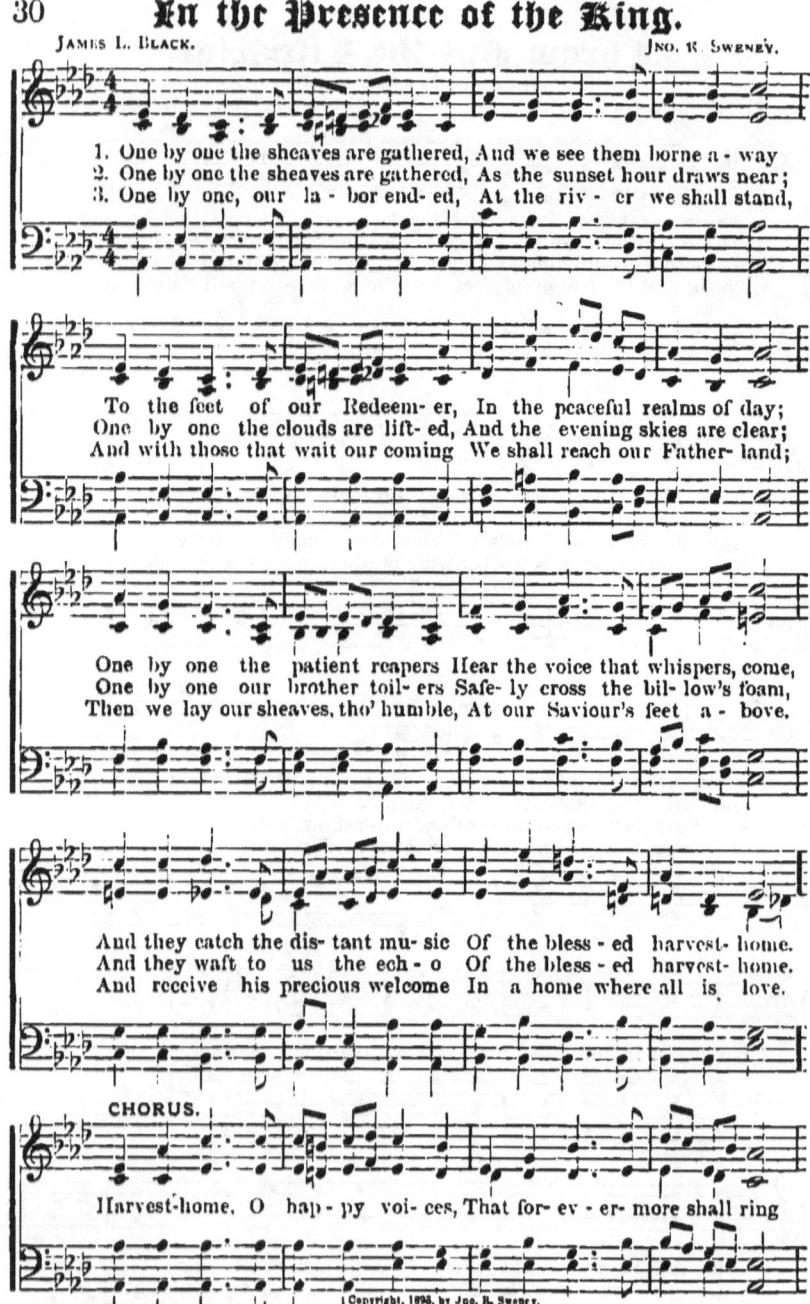

In the Presence, etc.—CONCLUDED.

Harvest-home a-mong the an-gels, In the presence of the King.

Waiting for You.

MARTHA J. LANKTON.   WM. J. KIRKPATRICK.

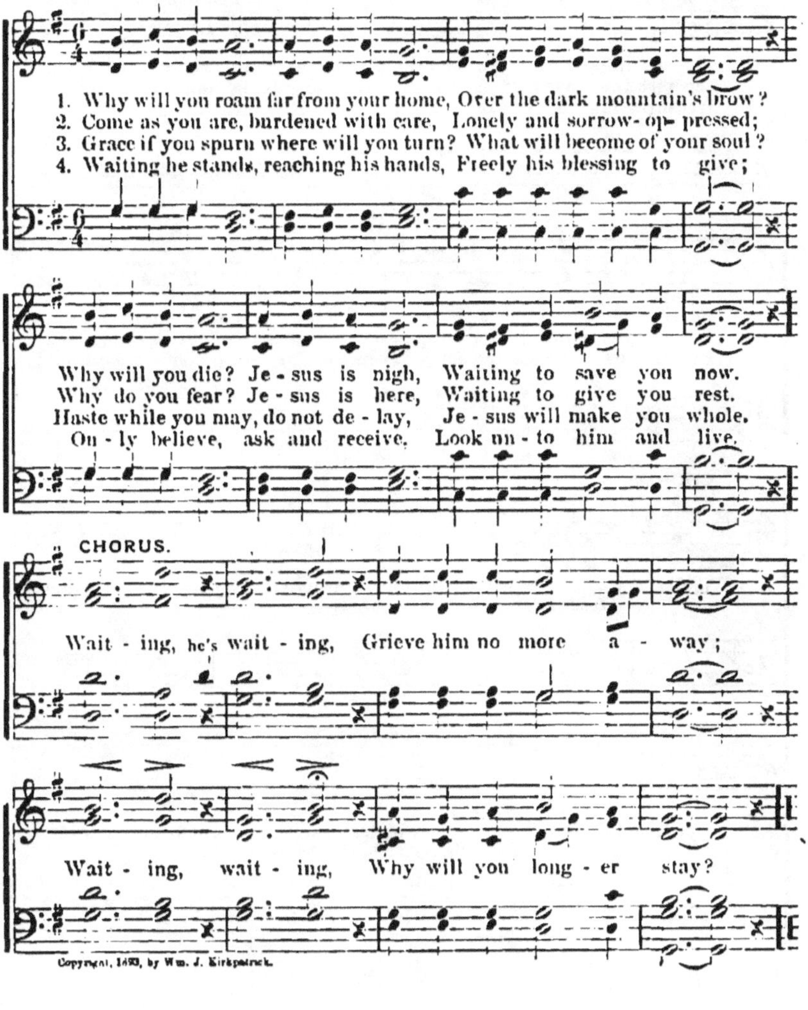

1. Why will you roam far from your home, Over the dark mountain's brow?
2. Come as you are, burdened with care, Lonely and sorrow-op-pressed;
3. Grace if you spurn where will you turn? What will become of your soul?
4. Waiting he stands, reaching his hands, Freely his blessing to give;

Why will you die? Je-sus is nigh, Waiting to save you now.
Why do you fear? Je-sus is here, Waiting to give you rest.
Haste while you may, do not de-lay, Je-sus will make you whole.
On-ly believe, ask and receive. Look un-to him and live.

CHORUS.

Wait-ing, he's wait-ing, Grieve him no more a-way;
Wait-ing, wait-ing, Why will you long-er stay?

Copyright, 1893, by Wm. J. Kirkpatrick.

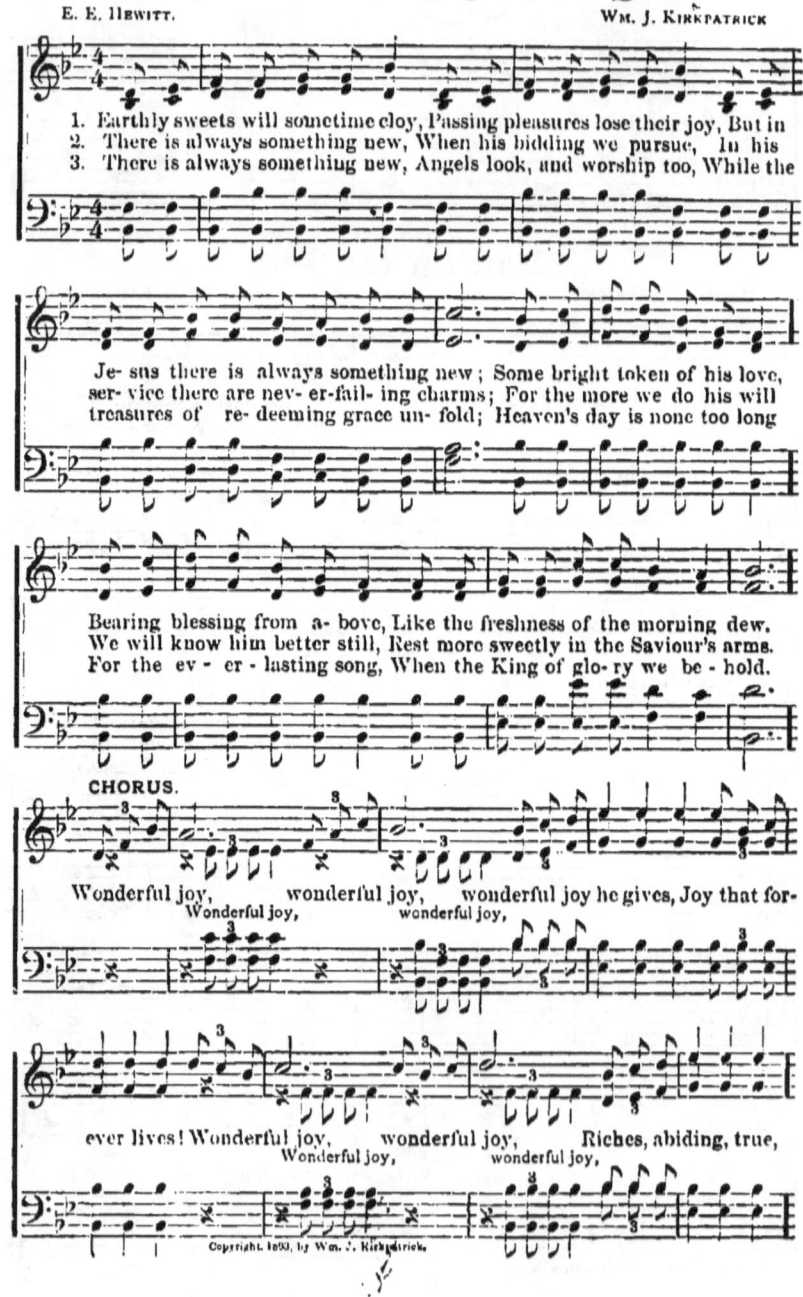

Always Something New, etc.—CONCLUDED. 33

Always in Jesus new, Wonderful joy, wonderful joy.
Wonderful joy, wonderful joy.

Invocation.

Rev H. J. ZELLEY.   H. L. GILMOUR.

Slowly.

1. Again we come with songs of praise, To him whose goodness crowns our days;
2. Come, save us from our bos - om sin, May all be clean without, within;
3. Our all is on the al - tar laid, A per- fect con- se- cration made;
4. Now answer prayer, and let us see Times of refreshing, Lord, from thee;

Fine.

In Christian fel - lowship we meet, To wor- ship at our Saviour's feet.
Take from us all un - ho - ly pride, May we with Christ be cru- cified.
Come here, O God, this ver - y hour, And seal us by thy Spirit's power.
Like floods let thy sal - vation roll, And pur - i - fy each waiting soul.

D. S.—Come, satis - fy our heart's desire, And send the Pen - te- cos - tal fire.

D. S.

Come, Ho - ly Spir - it, meet us here, And may we know that thou art near;

Copyright, 1893, by H. L. Gilmour   *Praise in Song*-C

Tell to the Nations.

37

"Go ye into all the world, and preach my gospel to every creature."—Jesus.

IDA L. REED.   H. L. GILMOUR.

1. Go tell to the nations in darkness, The story of wonderful love;
2. Go tell them of Jesus their Saviour, How much he hath borne for their sake;
3. Go tell them the beautiful sto-ry Of heaven's fair cit-y of light,

Christ died for their many transgressions, And promised a mansion a-bove.
How dearly and fondly he loves them, Bids all from their darkness awake.
How they may inher-it its glo-ry, And walk with the angels in white.

REFRAIN.

Go tell to the nations, Tell to the nations in darkness, Go tell to the nations, of
Tell to the nations in darkness, Go tell, go tell, Tell to the nations in darkness, of

Jesus the mighty to save; Go tell to the nations of him who hath borne all our
Tell who hath borne all our sorrows, Go tell

sorrows, Go tell, go tell, He's victor o'er death and the grave.
Go tell, Tell who hath borne all our sor-rows, He's

Copyright, 1893, by H. L. Gilmour.

40. My Father's Care.

H. L. G.
H. L. Gilmour.

1. There's not a bird that wings its flight, Nor li-ly blooms to ravish sight,
2. There's not a blade of grass that springs, Or feathered orchestra that sings,
3. There's not an eagle cleaves the sky. With stalwart wing and flashing eye,
4. There's not a soul, however vile, On whom the Saviour will not smile,

But in the song and perfume rare An ech-o whispers, Father's care.
But praises God, in earth and air, For dai-ly bread, for Father's care.
But from his fortress high in air Re-ech-oes back, my Father's care.
And now invites to gospel fare, To grace bestowed, and Father's care.

CHORUS.

My Father's care, my Father's care, Oh, blessed thought, without com'pare!
Those watchful eyes, that sparrows see, Will ne'er forget a child like me.

Copyright, 1893, by H. L. Gilmour.

5 There's not a soul who's born of God,
Has peace and pardon thro' the blood,
But in the hour of dark despair
Finds comfort, joy, in Father's care.

6 Speak forth, O flower, divinely clad,
And happy bird, with twitter glad,
And soul redeemed, boldly declare
We cannot doubt our Father's care.

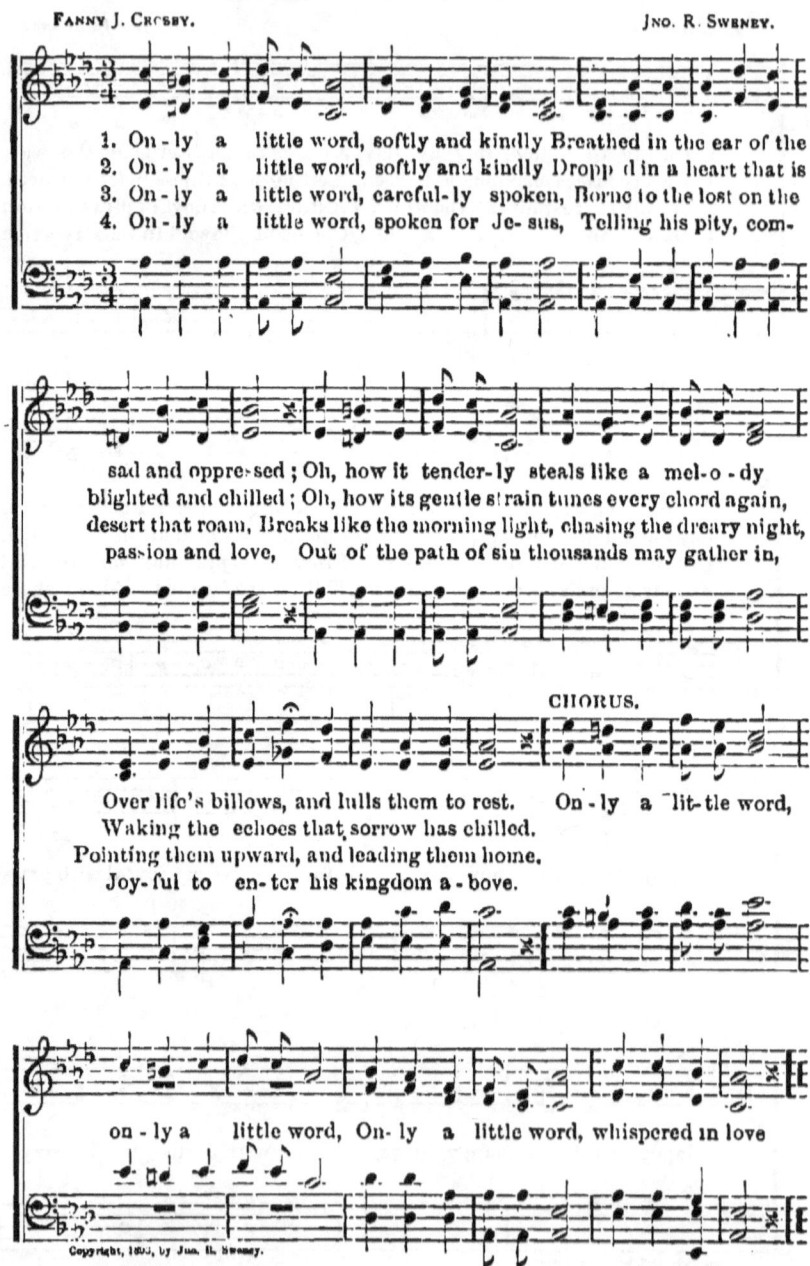

Oh, such Wonderful Love!

45

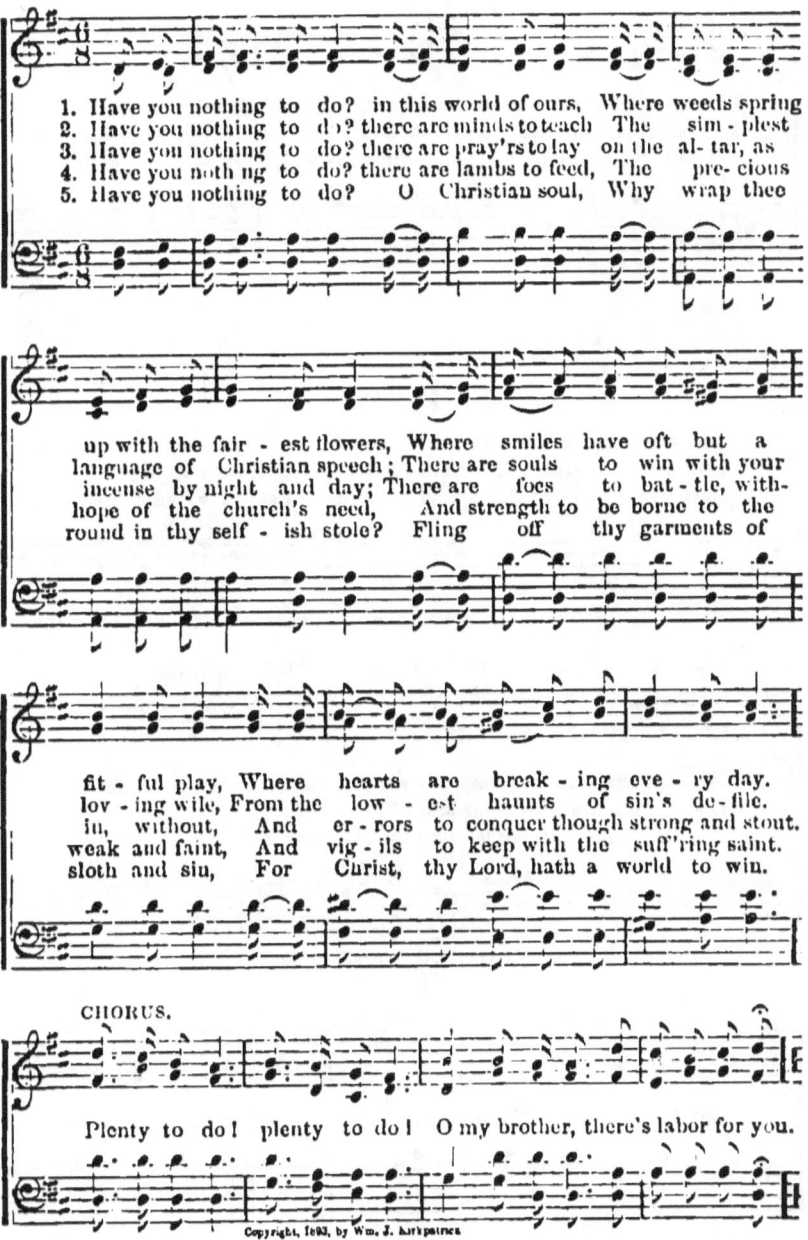

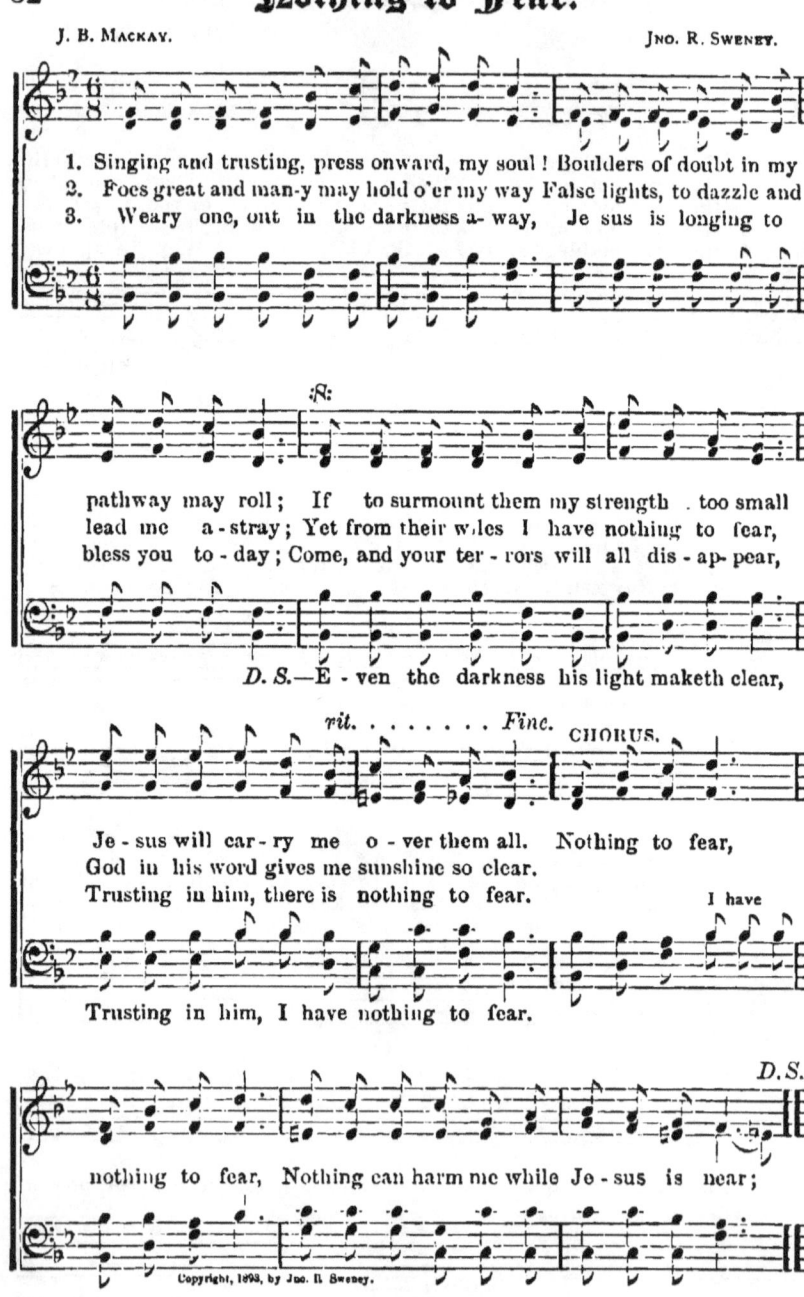

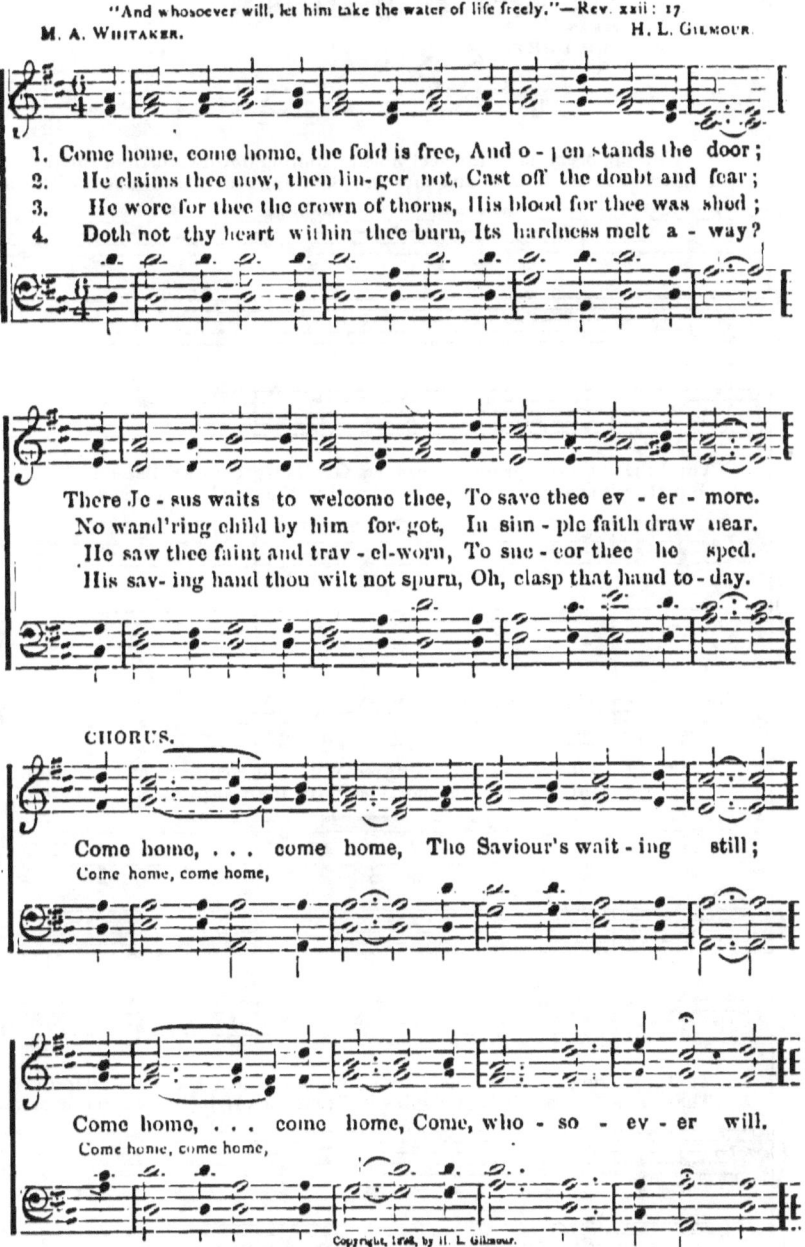

4 E'er since by faith I saw the stream
Thy flowing wounds supply,
Redeeming love has been my theme,
And shall be till I die.

5 Then in a nobler, sweeter song
I'll sing thy power to save,
When this poor lisping, stamm'ring
Lies silent in the grave. [tongue

Building Day by Day.—CONCLUDED. 61

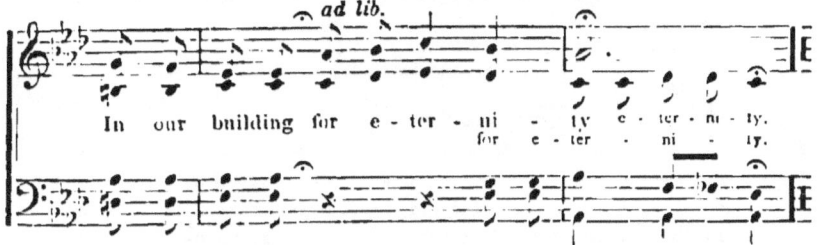

Jehovah, My Saviour.

Rev. R. M. McCheyne.   Wm. J. Kirkpatrick.

1. I once was a stranger to grace and to God; I knew not my danger and
2. When free grace awoke me by light from on high, Then legal fears shook me; I
3. My terrors all vanished before the sweet name; My guilty fears banished, with
4. Jehovah, the Lord, is my treasure and boast; Jehovah, my Saviour, I
5. E'en treading the valley, the shadow of death, This watchword shall rally my

felt not my load; Tho' friends spoke in rapture of Christ on the tree, Jehovah, my
trembled to die; No ref- uge, no safety, in self could I see; Jehovah! thou
boldness I came To drink at the fountain life-giving and free; Jehovah, my
ne'er can be lost; In thee I shall conquer by flood and by field, Jehovah, my
faltering breath; For while from life's fever my God sets me free, Jehovah, my

Saviour, was nothing to me, Je- hovah, my Saviour, was nothing to me.
on- ly my Saviour must be, Je- hovah, thou only my Saviour must be.
Saviour, is all things to me, Je- hovah, my Saviour, is all things to me.
anchor, Jehovah, my shield, Je- hovah, my anchor, Je- hovah, my shield!
Saviour, my death-song shall be, Jehovah, my Saviour, my death-song shall be!

Copyright, 1893, by Wm. J. Kirkpatrick.

62 Will You Meet Me in the Morning?

Lidie E. Hewitt.
Wm. J. Kirkpatrick.

SOLO, DUET OR QUARTET.

1. Will you meet me in the morning, When the shadows pass a-way?
2. Here the joy-beams, pure and tender, Oft are veiled by sorrow's night,
3. Je-sus, there, is all the glo-ry, Brighter than the sun his face;
4. See, oh, see, the golden dawn-ing Of the grand, e-ter-nal day!

When the glad and golden dawning Melts in-to the per-fect day.
But no clouds will dim the splendor Of the ev-er-last-ing light.
There we'll sing salvation's sto-ry, Sing the wonders of his grace.
Will you meet me in the morning, When the shadows pass a-way?

CHORUS.

Will you meet me in the morning? I'll be watching, I'll be waiting for you
Will you meet me, will you meet me in the morning? I'll be

there; Will you meet me in the morning, In that city bright and fair?
waiting for you there; Will you meet me, will you meet me in the morning,

Copyright, 1893, by Wm. J. Kirkpatrick.

Will You be Among the Number? 63

ALICE. M. LOWE. N. S. HOWARD.

1. Will you be among the number That shall hear the Saviour say,—
2. Will you be among the number That shall have a home at last
3. Will you be among the number That shall wear a robe of white,
4. Will you be among the number That make up the blood-wash'd throng,

"Well done, good and faithful servant," When he comes on judgment day?
With the Saviour and his loved ones, Where all pain and death are past?
That shall bear a harp in glo - ry, And be crowned with jewels bright?
Who both day and night with gladness Sing the ev - er - lasting song?

CHORUS.

Yes, I'll be among the number, Je-sus wants me to be
Yes, I'll be Jesus wants

there; He has paid the precious ransom, That his glo - ry I may share.

Copyright, 1887, by Joshua Gill.

Give Praise to God.

E. A. Barnes.   Wm. J. Kirkpatrick.

1. Give praise to God, who rules the earth and sky, And we behold his wonders far and near; Give praise to him whose eye is o-ver all, And who is good to all his children here.
2. Give praise to God, whose blessings freely flow, To make us glad with each return-ing day; Give praise to him whose all-suf-ficient grace Will keep us here from every e-vil way.
3. Give praise to God, who doeth all things well, And who is rich in mer-cy and in love; Give praise to him, for in his on-ly Son We all have life, e-ternal life a-bove.

CHORUS.

Give praise, give praise, With joy-ful notes give thanks and praise to God; Give praise, give praise, With grateful hearts give thanks and praise to God.

Copyright, 1893, by Wm J. Kirkpatrick.

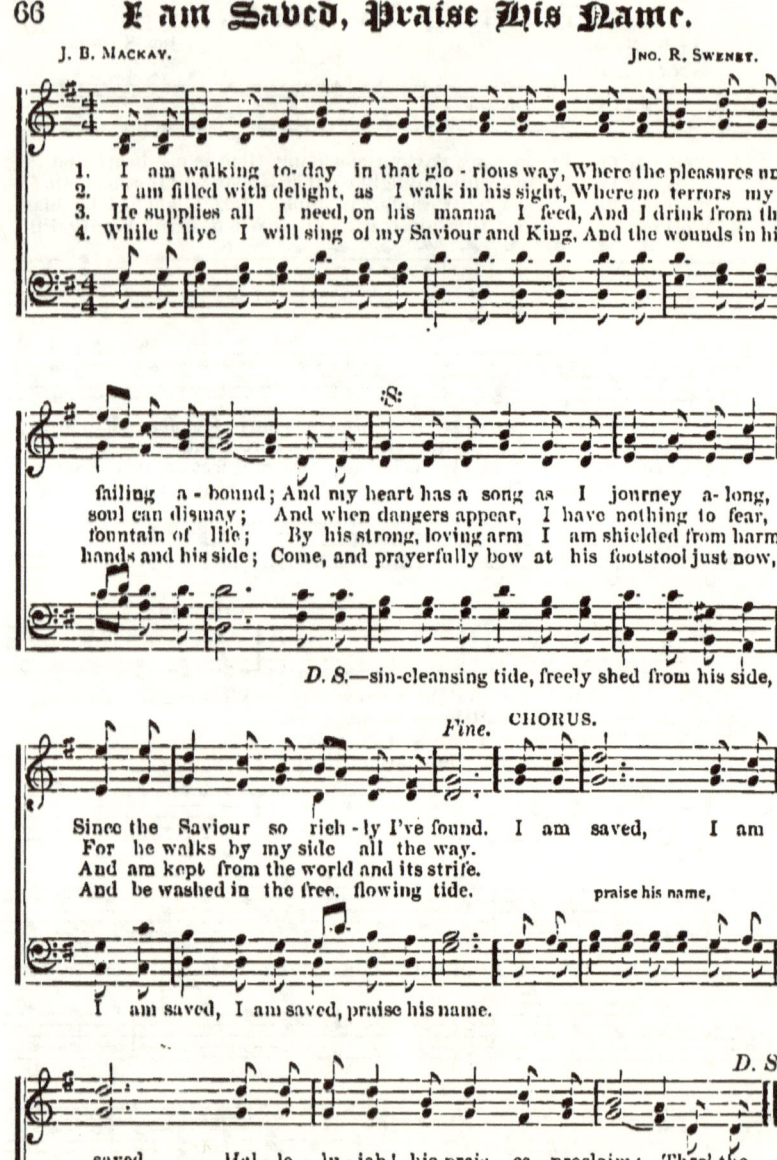

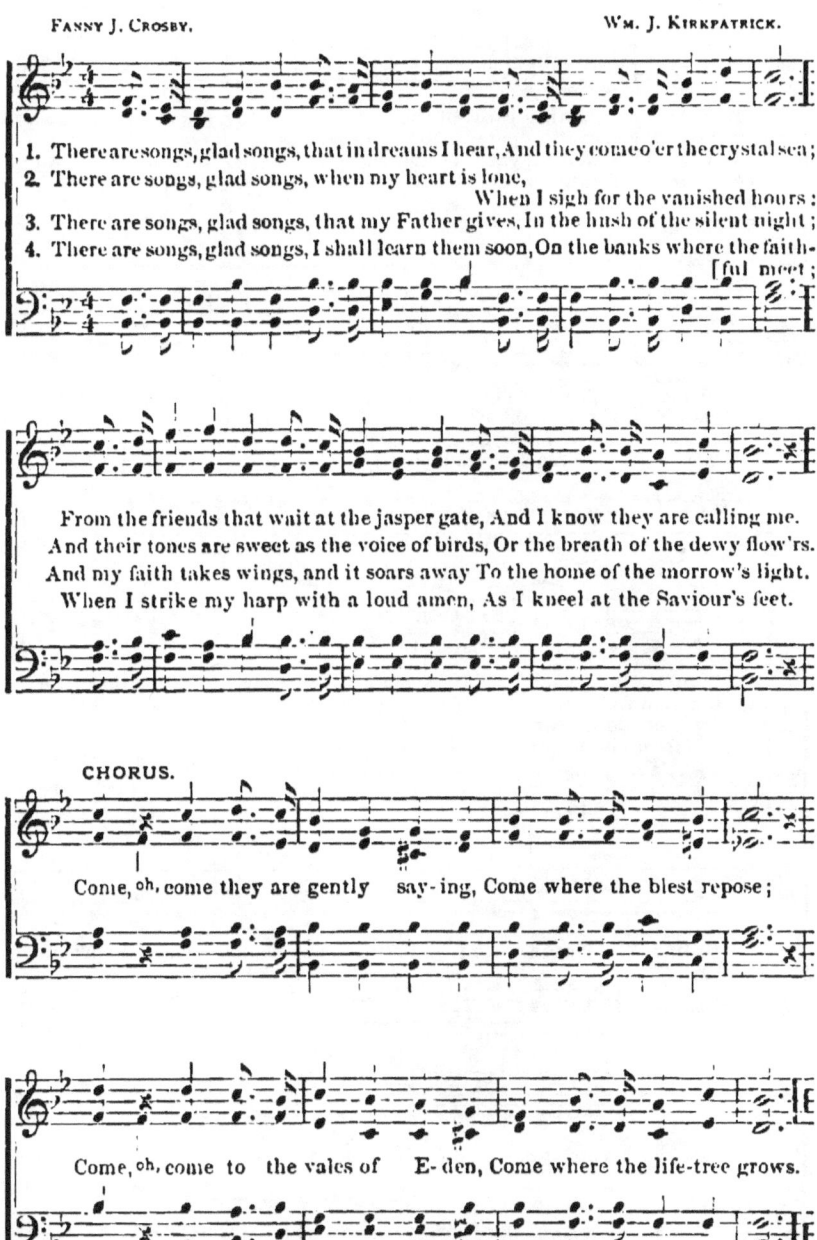

He Took My Place.

E. E. Hewitt.
Jno. R. Sweney.

1. A trembling soul, I sought the Lord, My sin confessed, my guilt deplored;
2. Here rests my heart; assurance sweet, His blessed work he will complete,
3. When sorrow veils the smiling day, When e-vil foes be-set my way,
4. No room for doubt, no room for fears, When to my view the cross appears,

How soft and sweet, his word to me, "I took thy place, and died for thee."
Since in his love, so great and free, He took my place, and died for me.
A-bundant grace in him I see, He took my place, and died for me.
My joy-ful song shall ev-er be, He took my place, and died for me.

CHORUS.

No oth-er hope .... no oth-er plea; .... He took my place, ... and died for me: .... O precious Lamb ... of Calva-ry! .... He took my place, ... and died for me. ....

Copyright, 1891, by Jno. R. Sweney.

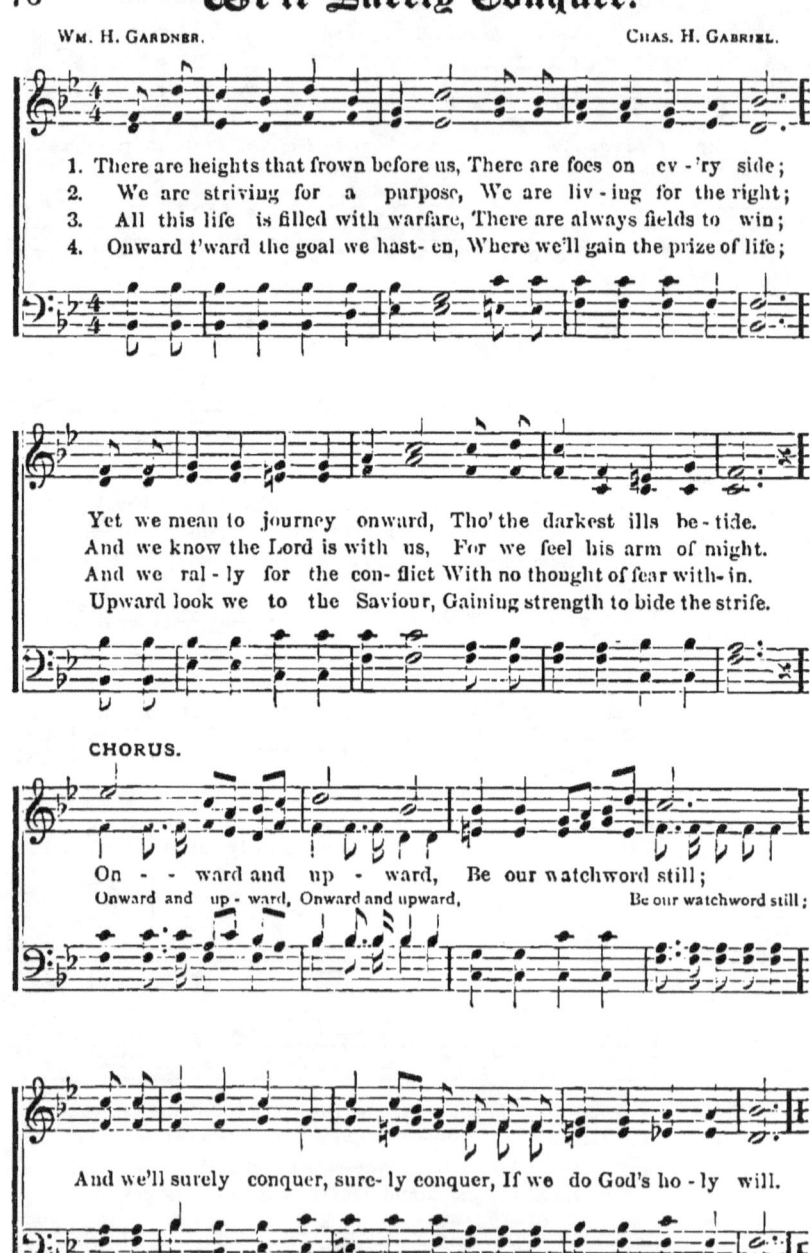

The Lord Dwelleth in Zion.

Rev. H. J. Zelley.   Joel iii: 21.   Wm. J. Kirkpatrick.

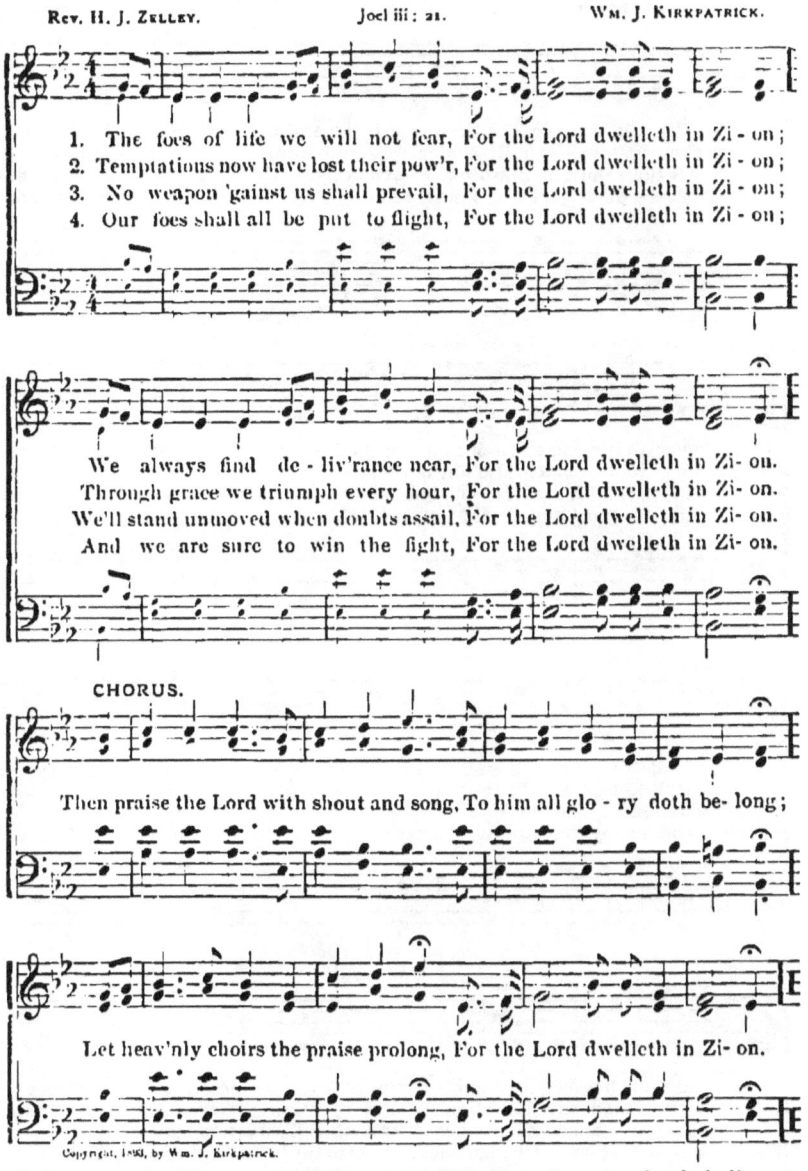

1. The foes of life we will not fear, For the Lord dwelleth in Zi-on;
2. Temptations now have lost their pow'r, For the Lord dwelleth in Zi-on;
3. No weapon 'gainst us shall prevail, For the Lord dwelleth in Zi-on;
4. Our foes shall all be put to flight, For the Lord dwelleth in Zi-on;

We always find de-liv'rance near, For the Lord dwelleth in Zi-on.
Through grace we triumph every hour, For the Lord dwelleth in Zi-on.
We'll stand unmoved when doubts assail, For the Lord dwelleth in Zi-on.
And we are sure to win the fight, For the Lord dwelleth in Zi-on.

CHORUS.

Then praise the Lord with shout and song, To him all glo-ry doth be-long;
Let heav'nly choirs the praise prolong, For the Lord dwelleth in Zi-on.

Copyright, 1893, by Wm. J. Kirkpatrick.

5 Our every need is now supplied,
  For the Lord dwelleth in Zion;
There's naught that we can ask beside,
  For the Lord dwelleth in Zion.

6 We will not fear when death shall come,
  For the Lord dwelleth in Zion;
And he will guide us safely home,
  For the Lord dwelleth in Zion.

Hallelujahs we'll Sing.—CONCLUDED.

join as one fold in communion so sweet, Hallelujahs we'll sing to his name.
sheep of his flock he guards safe night and day, Hallelujahs we'll sing to his name.
wanderers, come, there your hearts will o'erflow, And from all hallelujahs will ring.
hosts there in glory, to sing evermore Hallelujahs to Jesus' dear name.

CHORUS.

Sing hallelujahs, sing hallelujahs, Sing hal- lelujahs to his name;
Halle- lujahs to his name;

Hal - le - lujahs, hal - le - lujahs, Hal - le - lujahs we'll sing to his name.

Nothing to Pay.

L. H. Edmunds. Wm. J. Kirkpatrick.

1. Nothing to pay, for atonement's made, The blood has been shed, and the debt is paid.
2. Nothing to pay, for the blotted scroll Was nail'd to the cross where he sav'd my soul.
3. Nothing to pay, yet my all I owe Unto the dear Lord who hath loved me so.
4. Nothing to pay, but myself I'll bring To serve him forever, my Saviour King.
5. Nothing to pay, but my heart is his, 'Tis his who hath bought me for endless bliss.
6. Nothing to pay, but our thanks we'll raise, With rapture we'll render immortal [praise.

CHORUS.

Nothing to pay, nothing to pay, For Jesus has taken my debt away.

Copyright, 1886, by Wm. J. Kirkpatrick.

The Cross is my Anchor.

Wm. J. Coniver.   Jno. R. Sweney.

1. Tho' waves dash around me, no danger I fear, A bright star is shining, life's o-cean to cheer; I heed not the billows, for still I can sing, The cross is my anchor, and there will I cling.
2. Tho' waves dash around me, and loud thunders roll, The Lord is the refuge and strength of my soul; I dread not the tempest, for still I can sing, The cross is my anchor, and there will I cling.
3. Tho' waves dash around me, and wild is the gale, Tho' spars may be broken, and shattered the sail, No storms can ap-pal me, for still I can sing, The cross is my anchor, and there will I cling.
4. Tho' waves dash around me, yet, onward I go, Since Jesus has promised they shall not o'erflow; I smile at their rag-ing, for still I can sing, The cross is my anchor, and there will I cling.

CHORUS.

There will I cling, there will I cling, The cross is my anchor, and there will I cling; Oh, soon in the harbor at rest will I sing; The cross is my anchor, and Je-sus my King.

Praise in Song—F   Copyright, 1881, by Jno. R. Sweney.

84. The Wonderful Saviour.

Rev. H. J. Zelley.   "His name shall be called Wonderful."—Isa. ix: 6.   H. L. Gilmour.

1. Wea-ry and sinsick and read-y to die, Man raised to heav-en a
2. Je-sus our sorrows with pit-y did see, Left his bright home for to
3. He who for sinners his life freely gave, Won-der-ful, Counsel-lor,
4. Battles when o-ver, and ended life's days, Then with the ransomed our

pen-i-tent eye; God, moved to pit-y by man's hopeless cry,
die on the tree; Purchased sal-va-tion for you and for me,
might-y to save, Gives us the vic-t'ry o'er death and the grave;
voic-es we'll raise, Hearts full of glad-ness for-ev-er will praise

CHORUS.

Sent us a won-der-ful Sav-iour. Help me, O broth-ers, the
Oh, what a won-der-ful Sav-iour!
He is a won-der-ful Sav-iour.
Je-sus, our won-der-ful Sav-iour.

sto-ry to tell, Help me, O sis-ters, his praises to swell; Honor the

One who has loved us so well, Je-sus, our won-der-ful Sav-iour.

Copyright, 1893, by H. L. Gilmour.

We are Singing On the Way.

L. H. Edmunds.   Chas. Edw. Pollock.

1. We are sing-ing on the way, To a blessed land of day, Where the raptured hal-le-lu-jahs nev-er cease; Soon we'll see its shining towers, Rest within its lovely bowers, In that Eden-land of ev-er-lasting peace.
2. What though trials here we meet? Soon we'll walk the golden street, Where we'll look up-on the beau-ty of our King; Tears of sorrow here may flow, But "hereafter we shall know," And redeeming love thro' endless ages sing.
3. We are pressing on the way, Let us work, and watch, and pray, Winning stars to sparkle in our crowns of light; Let us tell the Saviour's love, Till he bids us come above, Where no shadow ever mars the radiance bright.

D.S.—glory we shall share, In the house of "many mansions," bright and fair.

CHORUS.

Blessed home! blessed home! In the house of "many mansions," bright and fair; For we'll be like Je-sus there, And his

Copyright, 1891, by W. J. Kirkpatrick.

That Old, Old Story is True.—CONCLUDED. 95

found out the reason they love it so well, That old, old sto-ry is true.
oh, what sweet peace in my heart since I found That old, old sto-ry is true.
peace to my soul, it is joy to my heart That old, old sto-ry is true.
mansion in glo-ry for all who beleive" That old, old sto-ry is true.

REFRAIN.

That old, old sto-ry is true, That old, old sto-ry is true; But I've
That old, old sto-ry is .true, That old, old sto-ry is true; But
That old, old sto-ry is true, That old, old sto-ry is true; It is
That old, old sto-ry is true, That old, old sto-ry is true; "There's a
                                      it is true,   it is true,

found out the reason they love it so well, That old, old sto-ry is true.
oh, what sweet peace in my heart since I've found That old, old story is true.
peace to my soul, it is joy to my heart, That old, old sto-ry is true.
mansion in glo-ry for all who believe" That old, old sto-ry is true.

Home of the Soul.   Key Eb.

1 I will sing you a song of a beautiful land,
   The far-away home of the soul,
   Where no storms ever beat on the glittering strand,
   While the years of eternity roll. etc.

2 Oh, that home of the soul in my visions and dreams,
   Its bright, jasper walls I can see;
   Till I fancy but thinly the veil intervenes
   Between the fair city and me. etc.

3 That unchangeable home is for you and for me,
   Where Jesus of Nazareth stands;
   The King of all kingdoms forever is he,
   And he holdeth our crowns in his hands. etc.

4 Oh, how sweet it will be in that beautiful land,
   So free from all sorrow and pain,
   With songs on our lips, and with harps in our hands,
   To meet one another again. etc.

98. Dear Jesus, Canst Thou Help Me?

FANNY J. CROSBY.   WM. J. KIRKPATRICK.

1. Dear Je-sus, canst thou help me? My soul is full of woe;
2. I feel I am a sin-ner, And this my on-ly plea,
3. I've heard there is a fountain, Where cleansing wa-ters flow;
4. Thy blood doth fill that fountain, Thy blood so pure and free;
5. Dear Je-sus, lov-ing Saviour, Thou precious dy-ing Lamb,

My heart is al-most breaking, I've no-where else to go.
The sweet and blest as-sur-ance That thou hast died for me.
My sins, though red like crim-son, May now be white as snow.
That blood a-vailed for oth-ers, And now a-vails for me.
While here my faith is plead-ing, Now take me as I am.

CHORUS.

I've no-where else to go, Dear Je-sus, but to thee,
And so I lift my voice and cry, Have mer-cy, Lord, on me;

D.S.—And so I lift my voice and cry, Have mer-cy, Lord, on me.

Have mer-cy, Lord, on me, Have mer-cy, Lord, on me,

Copyright, 1890, by Wm. J. Kirkpatrick.

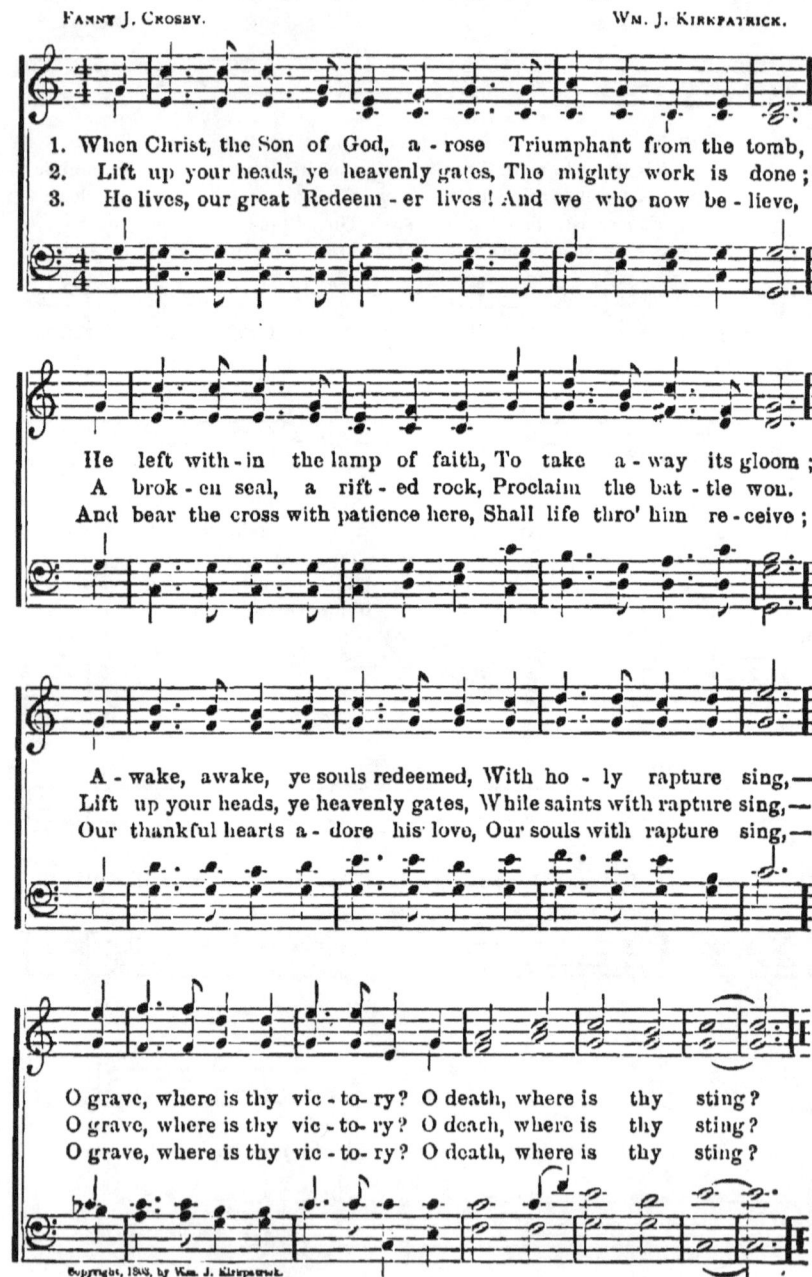

Rest Awhile.

107

Lizzie Edwards.
Jno. R. Sweney.

1. When faints the heart beneath the heavy burden Of human woes that cannot be suppressed; When anxious ones are coming still and going,
2. And there alone with Jesus on the mountain, What joy is ours, what visions of delight; Our faith mounts up as on the wings of eagles,
3. Yet not for aye the rest, the joy, the transport, The interchange of thought, as friend with friend; But, for the work we still have left unfinished
4. Thrice blessed mount of holy transformation, Where Jesus oft permits his own to stay; Oh, bliss to rise and breathe its air a moment!

And leave no time for leisure, calm or rest. How sweet the words that all our fears beguile, Come ye apart with me and rest awhile;
And soars at will from tow'ring height to height.
Our souls are strong when we again descend.
Then speed us on to everlasting day.

CHORUS.

How sweet the words that all our fears beguile, Come ye apart with me and rest awhile.

Copyright, 1887, by Jno. R. Sweney.

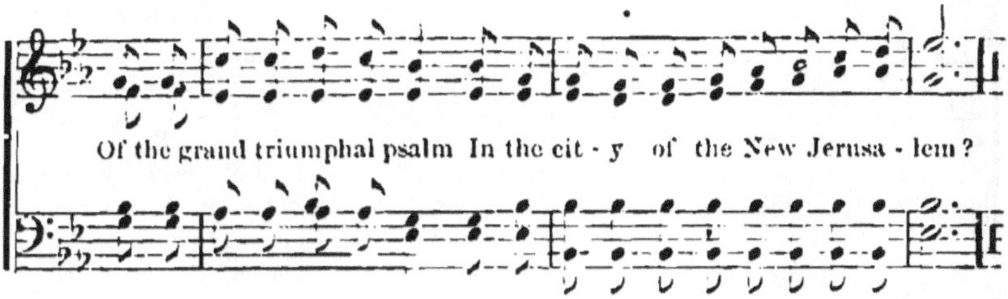

In the City.—CONCLUDED. 109

Of the grand triumphal psalm In the cit-y of the New Jerusa-lem?

Consolation.

"Blessed are they that mourn, for they shall be comforted."—Jesus.

M. A. WHITAKER.   H. L. GILMOUR.

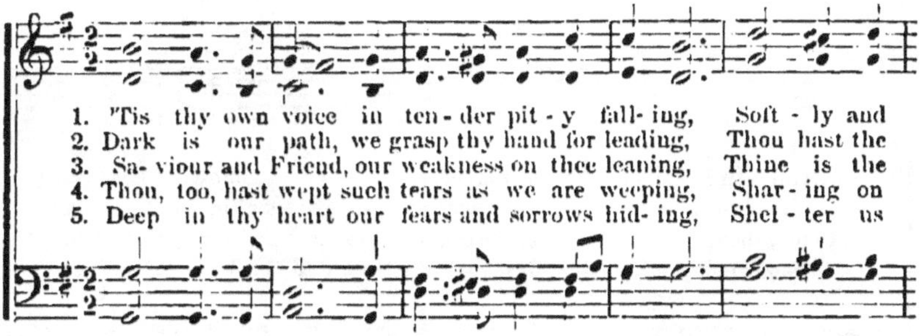

1. 'Tis thy own voice in ten-der pit-y fall-ing, Soft-ly and
2. Dark is our path, we grasp thy hand for leading, Thou hast the
3. Sa-viour and Friend, our weakness on thee leaning, Thine is the
4. Thou, too, hast wept such tears as we are weeping, Shar-ing on
5. Deep in thy heart our fears and sorrows hid-ing, Shel-ter us

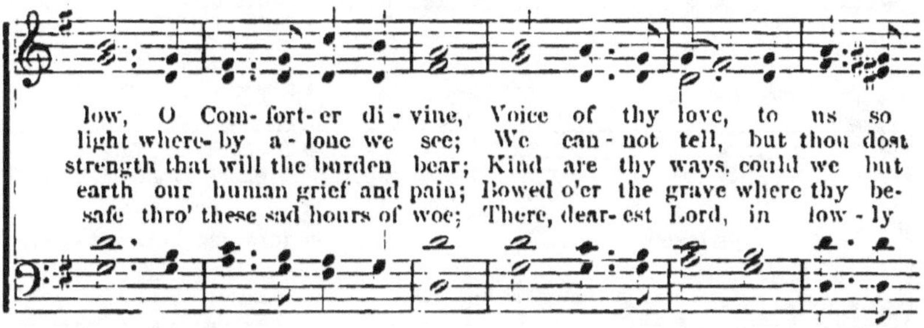

low, O Com-fort-er di-vine, Voice of thy love, to us so
light where-by a-lone we see; We can-not tell, but thou dost
strength that will the burden bear; Kind are thy ways, could we but
earth our human grief and pain; Bowed o'er the grave where thy be-
safe thro' these sad hours of woe; There, dear-est Lord, in low-ly

gent-ly call-ing, Bid-ding us rest our bruised hearts in thine.
own our needing, So we re-sign ourselves, our all to thee.
read their meaning, Did we but trust thy ev-er watch-ful care.
loved lay sleeping, Help us to pray, all oth-er help is vain.
faith a-bid-ing, Rest may we find, and tru-est com-fort know.

Copyright, 1878, by H. L. Gilmour.

If Ye Love Me.

Myron W. Morse.   Jno. R. Sweney.

1. "If ye love me," saith the Saviour, "If ye love me, feed my sheep,
2. "If ye love me," oh, how tender Is the voice of Jesus now,
3. We would love thee, blessed Saviour, We would hear thy voice to-day,
4. Lord, we love thee! wondrous sto-ry, Weak and sinful though we be,

And in heart and life re-member Ev-er my commandments keep."
"If ye love me, then re-member At the mer-cy-seat to bow."
Come, then, with thy lov-ing Spir-it, Bless us as we sing and pray.
Through redemption thou dost save us, Now and thro' e-ter-ni-ty.

CHORUS.

"If ye love me," saith the Saviour, "If ye love me, hear my voice,

Come, and in my words re-joicing, Make me your e-ter-nal choice."

Copyright, 1883, by Jno. R. Sweney.

116. The Song-Land.

Fanny J. Crosby.   Mrs. J. G. Wilson.

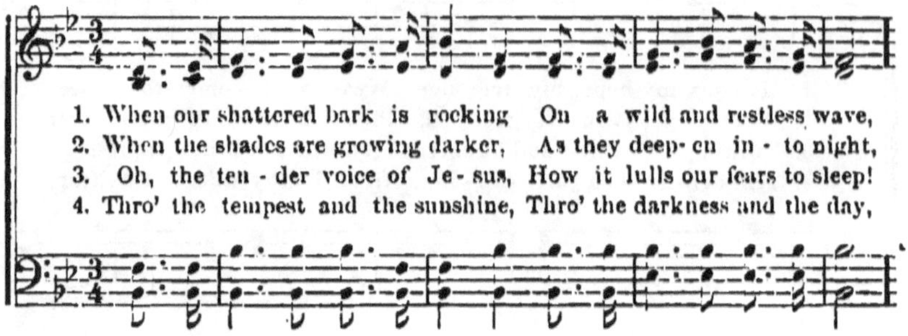

1. When our shattered bark is rocking On a wild and restless wave,
2. When the shades are growing darker, As they deep-en in-to night,
3. Oh, the ten-der voice of Je-sus, How it lulls our fears to sleep!
4. Thro' the tempest and the sunshine, Thro' the darkness and the day,

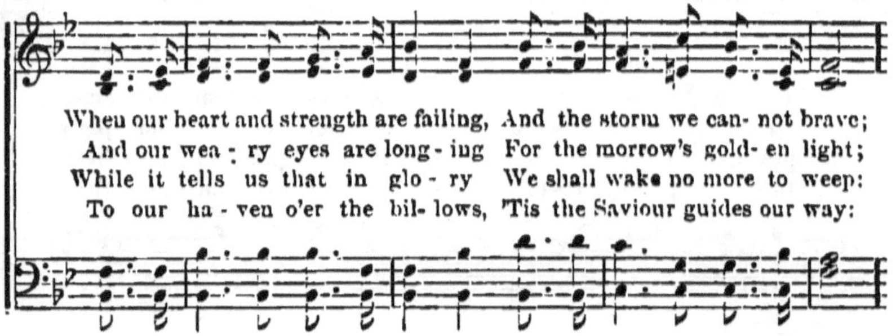

When our heart and strength are failing, And the storm we can-not brave;
And our wea-ry eyes are long-ing For the morrow's gold-en light;
While it tells us that in glo-ry We shall wake no more to weep:
To our ha-ven o'er the bil-lows, 'Tis the Saviour guides our way:

CHORUS.

Oh, the lov-ing words we hear, Like a whis-per soft and low,

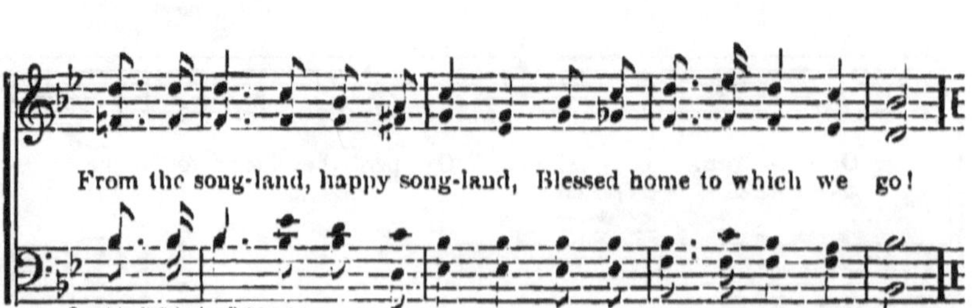

From the song-land, happy song-land, Blessed home to which we go!

Copyright, 1889, by Jno. R. Sweney.

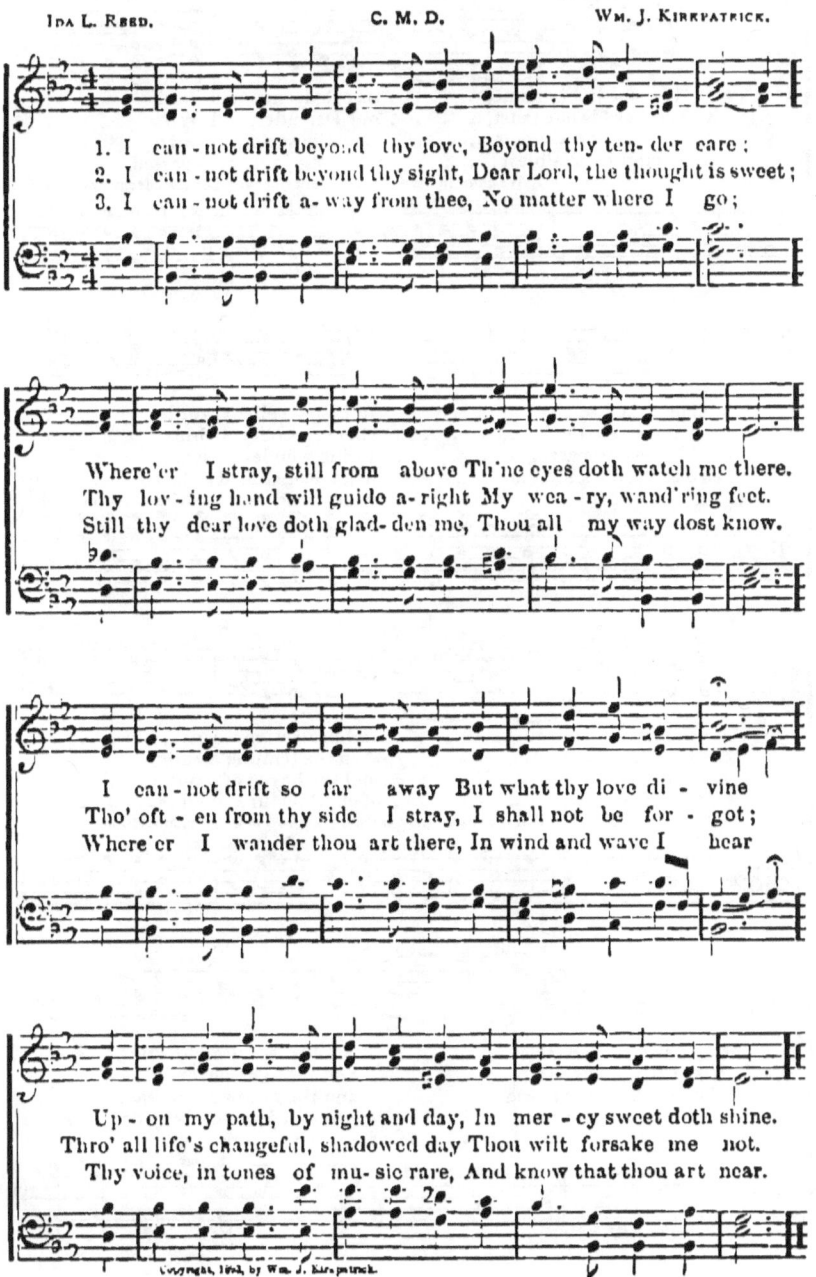

3 Thou art hungry, yet thy Father
  Hath a feast prepared for thee;
  Thou art thirsty, yet the fountain
  Of his love thou wilt not see.

4 Trav'ler, now the time accepted,
  Come thou quickly, haste away;
  There's no promise for the morrow,
  Mercy calls, and calls to-day.

I am Walking, etc.—CONCLUDED.

ev-ermore rejoice, For he's promised to go with me all the way.

Thou Art My Refuge.

IDA L. REED.   WM. J. KIRKPATRICK.

1. Thou art my refuge, dear Saviour, Thou art my strength and my shield;
2. Thou art my refuge, dear Saviour, All of my trust is in thee;
3. Thou art my refuge, dear Saviour, Thou my Redeem-er and Friend;

Thou art my hope and sal-va-tion, All un-to thee I will yield.
Un-der thy wings will I hide me, There will be safety for me.
Watching me e'er as I jour-ney, Walking with me to the end.

CHORUS.

Thou art my refuge, dear Saviour, Thou whom my heart holdeth dear;

Watching so lov-ing-ly o'er me, nev-er for-saking me here.

Copyright, 1898, by Wm. J. Kirkpatrick.

Oh, Master, Save.—CONCLUDED.

Save, or we perish, oh, Master, save, Thou King of wild Gali - lee.
Save, save,

Wash Me, O Lamb of God.

H. B. BEEGLE. Wm. J. KIRKPATRICK.

May be used as a Duett.

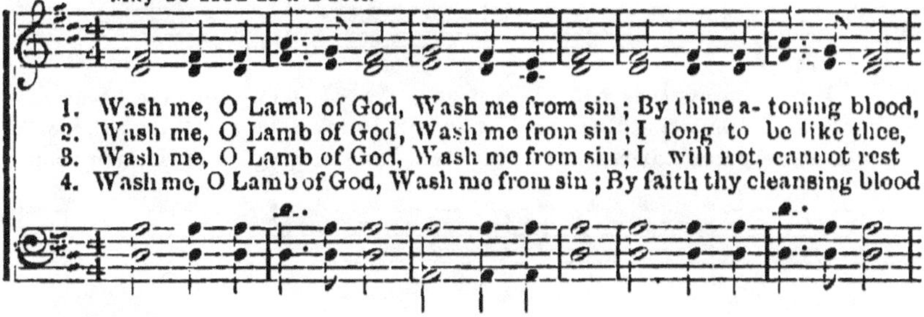

1. Wash me, O Lamb of God, Wash me from sin ; By thine a- toning blood,
2. Wash me, O Lamb of God, Wash me from sin ; I long to be like thee,
3. Wash me, O Lamb of God, Wash me from sin ; I will not, cannot rest
4. Wash me, O Lamb of God, Wash me from sin ; By faith thy cleansing blood

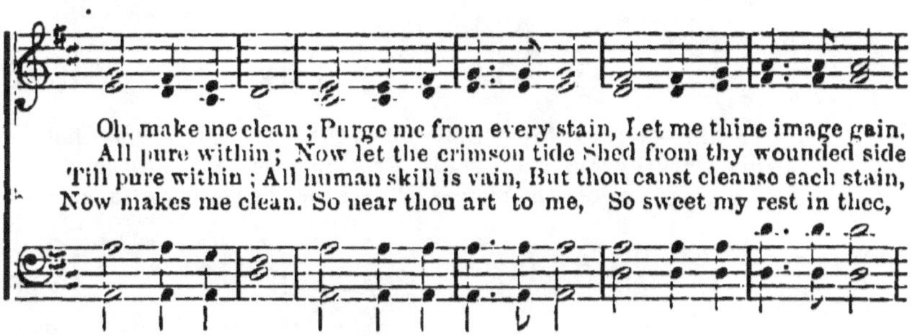

Oh, make me clean ; Purge me from every stain, Let me thine image gain,
All pure within ; Now let the crimson tide Shed from thy wounded side
Till pure within ; All human skill is vain, But thou canst cleanse each stain,
Now makes me clean. So near thou art to me, So sweet my rest in thee,

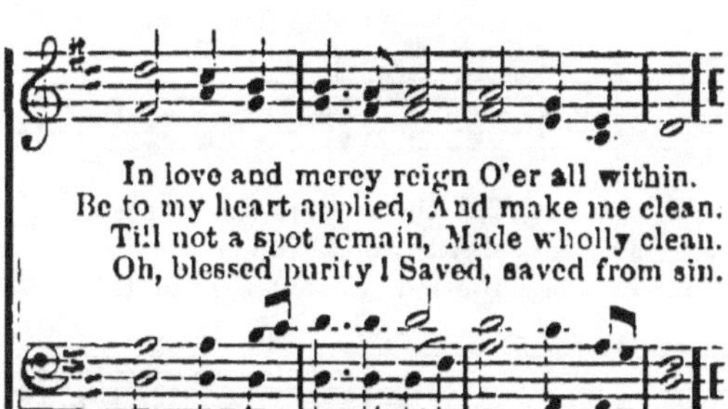

In love and mercy reign O'er all within.
Be to my heart applied, And make me clean.
Till not a spot remain, Made wholly clean.
Oh, blessed purity ! Saved, saved from sin.

5 Wash me, O Lamb of God,
 Wash me from sin ;
Thou, while I trust in thee,
 Wilt keep me clean ;
Each day to thee I bring
 Heart, life, yea, everything ;
Saved while to thee I cling,
 Saved from all sin.

Copyright, 1890, by Wm. J. Kirkpatrick.

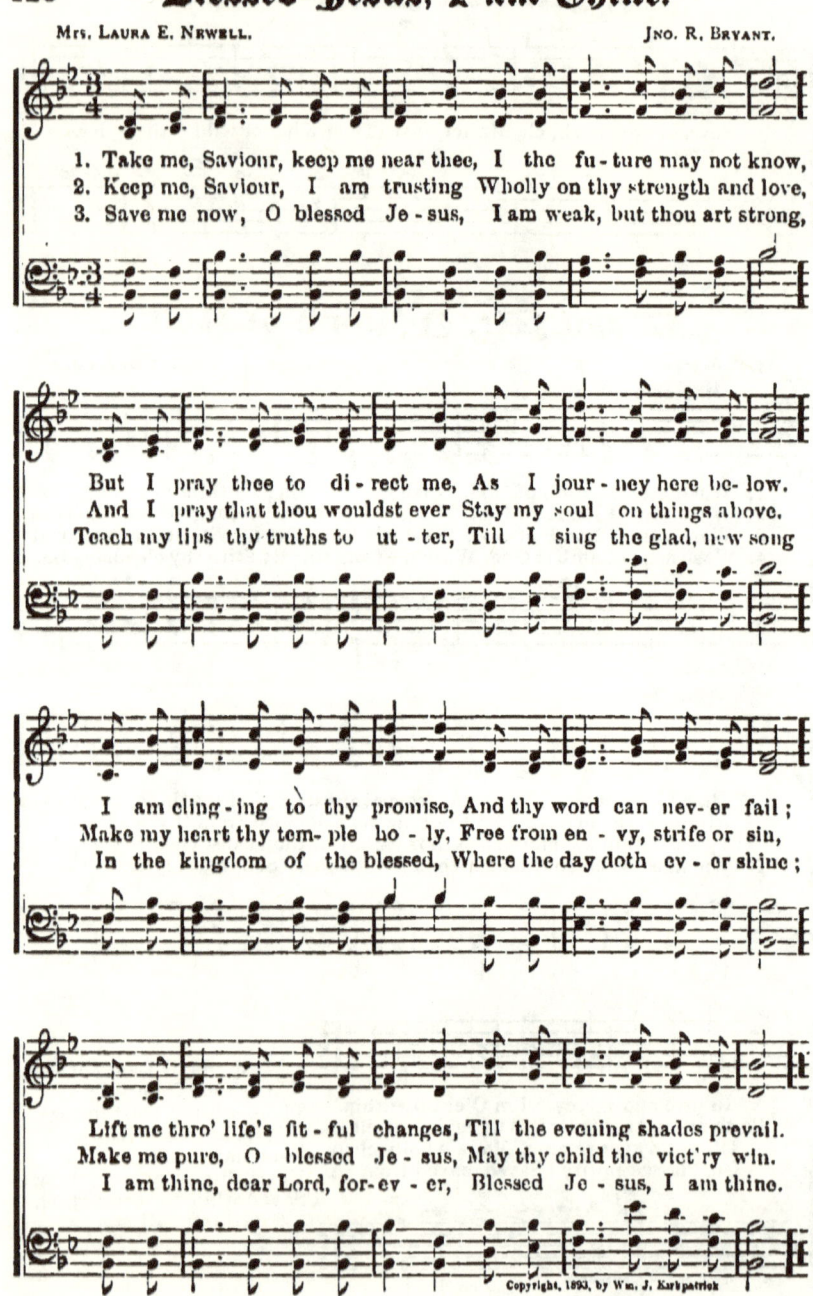

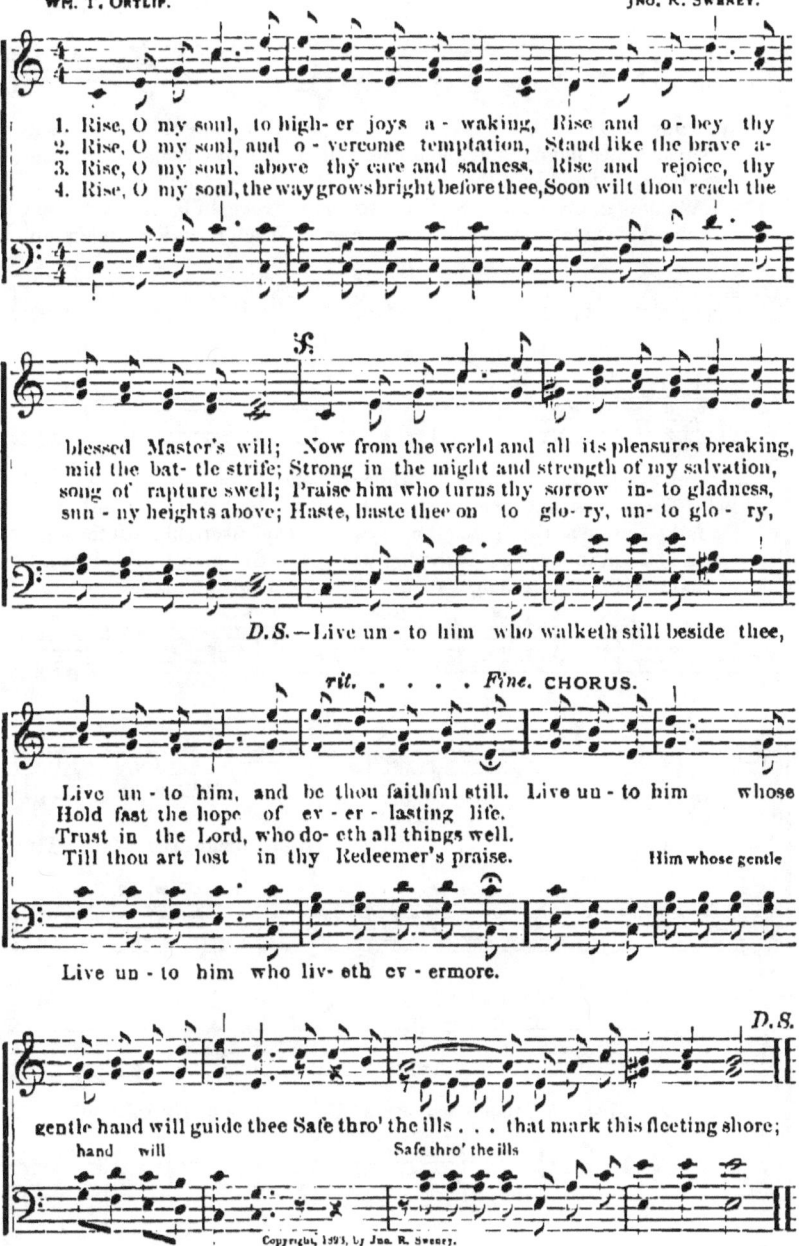

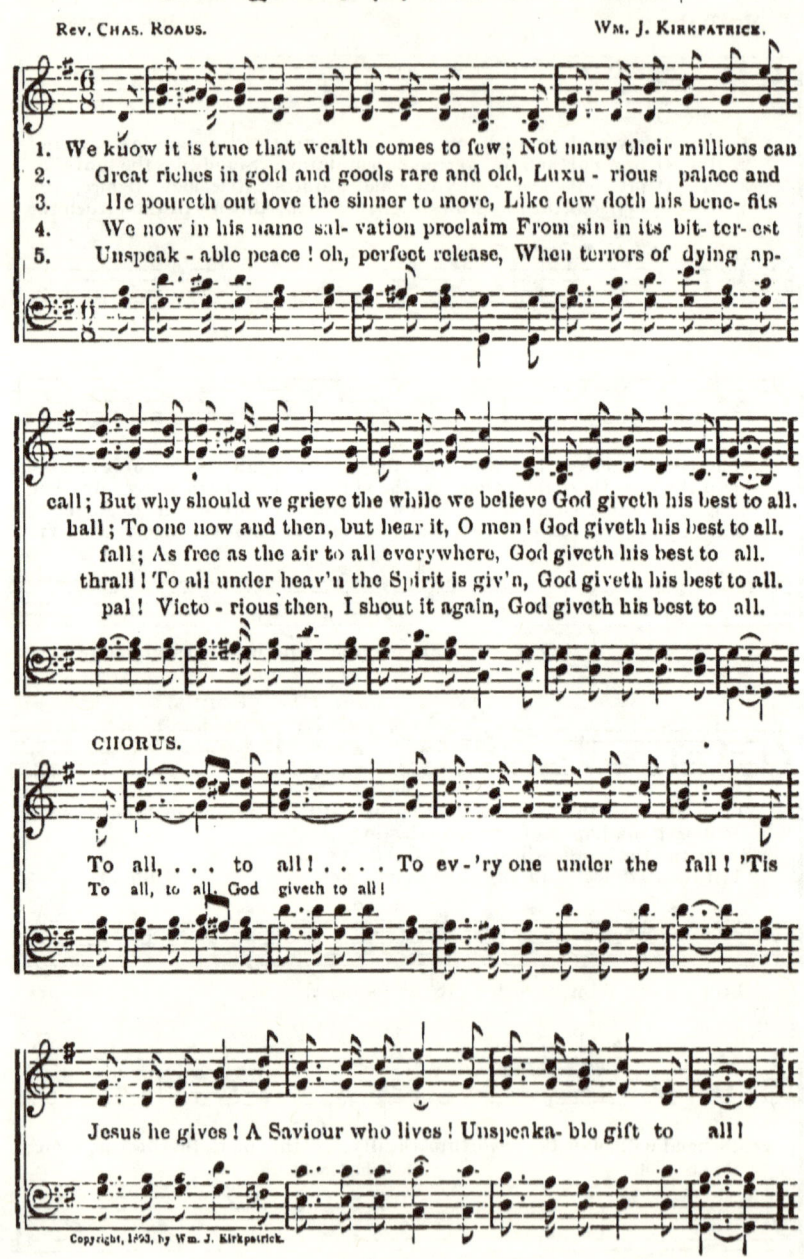

130. At Thy Feet.

M. A. Whitaker. — Job. xlii: 5, 6. — H. L. Gilmour.

1. At last, my King and Saviour, Thy face divine I see, As shining thro' the darkness, 'Tis bent in love on me; That patient look appeal-ing, Thy call so low and sweet, Have bowed me down in sorrow, Repentant, at thy feet.
2. Those feet, how worn and weary, As o'er this earth they sped, With hope to cheer the hopeless, And life to give the dead; Those feet for us so wounded, The nail-prints still are there, Yet joy was in thy suff'ring, And pardon in thy pray'r.
3. This load of sin—thou knowest, Its weight doth press me sore; Wilt thou not lift the burden, And hope and peace restore? I trust thy tender mercy, Thy sac-ri-fice I plead, Oh, grant me full forgivness, And help for coming need.
4. By all the wrong and torture Thou freely didst endure, Oh, take me in my weakness, And make me strong and pure; Thy life for me was giv-en, Let mine be true to thee, A life of loving service, From self and sin set free.

CHORUS.

At thy feet, at thy feet, Je-sus, now I bow; Speak that word, forgiven, Speak, oh, speak it now. Speak that word, forgiven, Speak, oh, speak it now.

Copyright, 1893, by H. L. Gilmour.

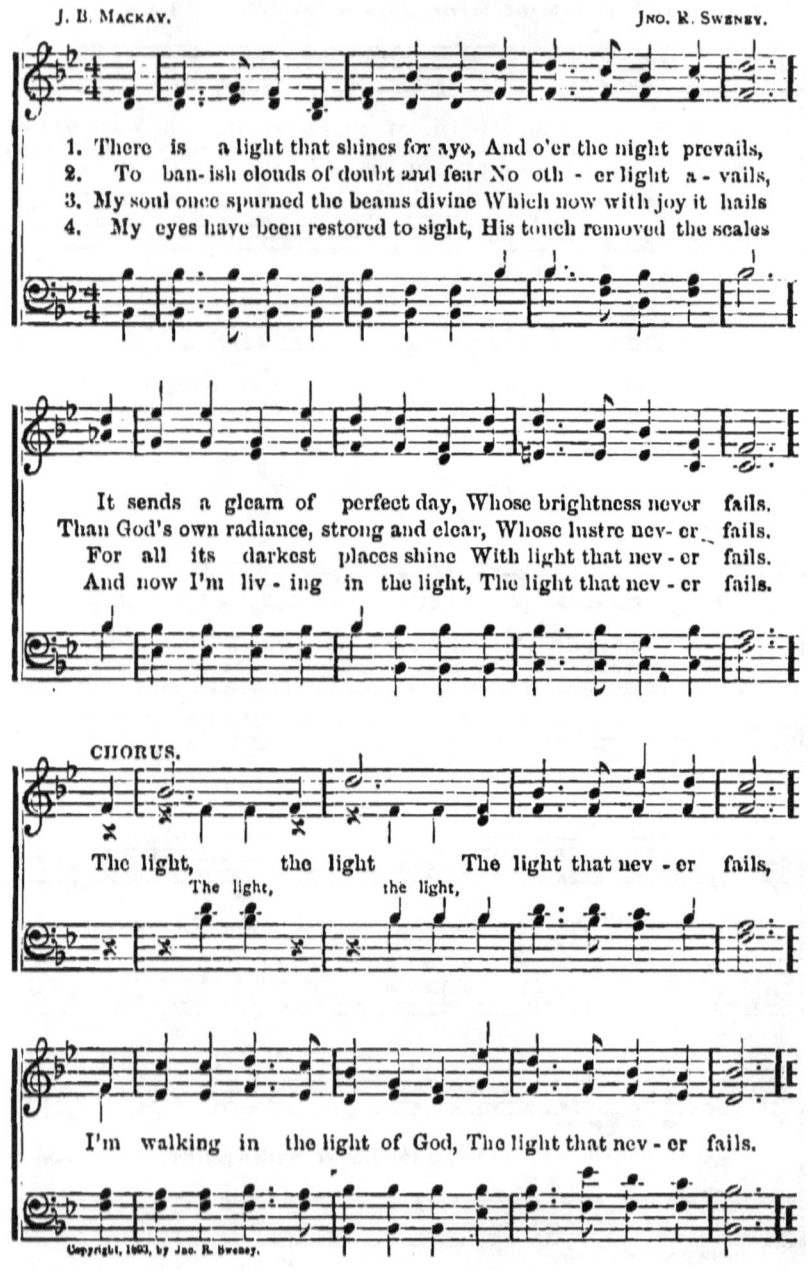

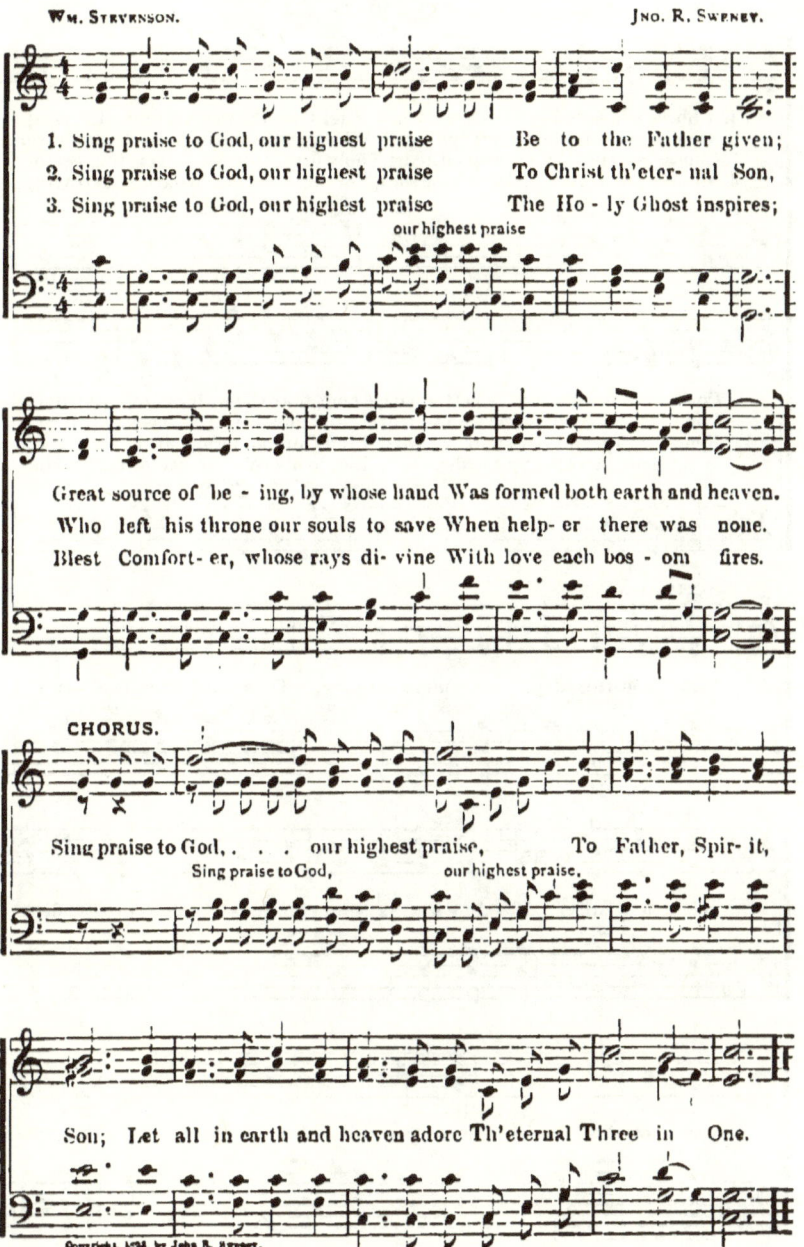

Do Not Make Light of the Call.

JAMES L. PLACK.   JNO. R. SWENEY.

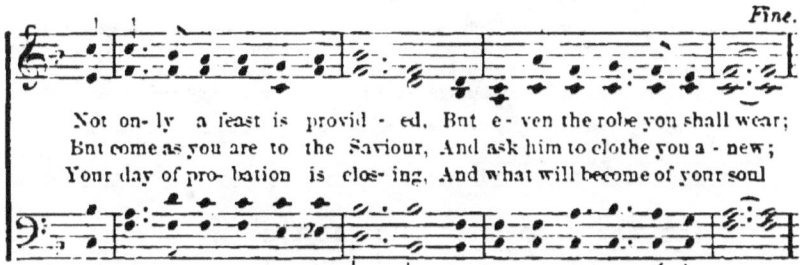

1. The Master commandeth his servants To go and the message declare.
2. You never can make yourselves better, There's nothing remaining to do.
3. But why are you making ex-cu-ses? Your moments, how swiftly they roll!

D.S.—come, for all things are now ready. Oh, do not make light of the call;

Not on-ly a feast is provid-ed, But e-ven the robe you shall wear;
But come as you are to the Saviour, And ask him to clothe you a-new;
Your day of pro-bation is clos-ing, And what will become of your soul

For these are the words of the Master, So urgent-ly spoken to all.

A feast of his love and sal-va-tion, A robe that is whiter than snow,
The debt of your sin he hath cancelled, The blood of atonement is free;
When summoned to stand at the judgment? Excu-ses will there be in vain.

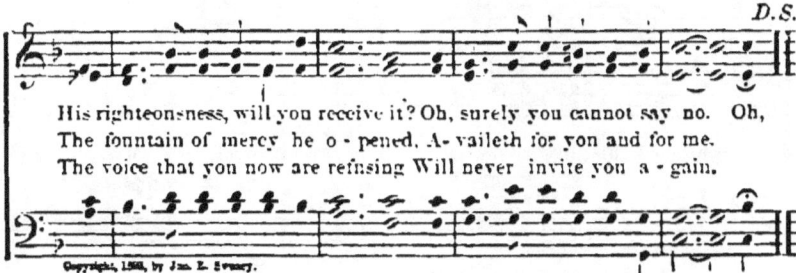

His righteousness, will you receive it? Oh, surely you cannot say no. Oh,
The fountain of mercy he o-pened, A-vaileth for you and for me.
The voice that you now are refusing Will never invite you a-gain.

Copyright, 1888, by Jno. R. Sweney.

The Everlasting Song

Emma M. Johnston. Wm. J. Kirkpatrick.

1. When the port of heaven o-pens to a world redeemed from sin,
2. There the harps shall thrill as harps were never known to thrill before,
3. And when ceaseless ages shall have passed, with a-ges yet to come.

When the great arch foe is vanquished, and the vic-tors en-ter in,
And no voic-es shall be si-lent on that safe and hap-py shore,
When from all of earth-ly sor-row free we rest with-in that home,

There will be a burst of triumph, like the sounding of the sea,—
But with glo-ri-ous commingling shall the mighty anthem swell,
Still the cho-rus shall be pealing forth, un-changing, grand and free:

Like the voice of ma-ny wa-ters shall that glorious anthem be:
To the King of kings, and Lord of lords, who hath done all things well.
"Un-to him who hath redeemed us let e-ter-nal glo-ry be!"

REFRAIN.

Glo-ry glo - - - ry to his name, Now and
Glo-ry to his name, glo-ry to his name,

Copyright, 1897, by Wm. J. Kirkpatrick.

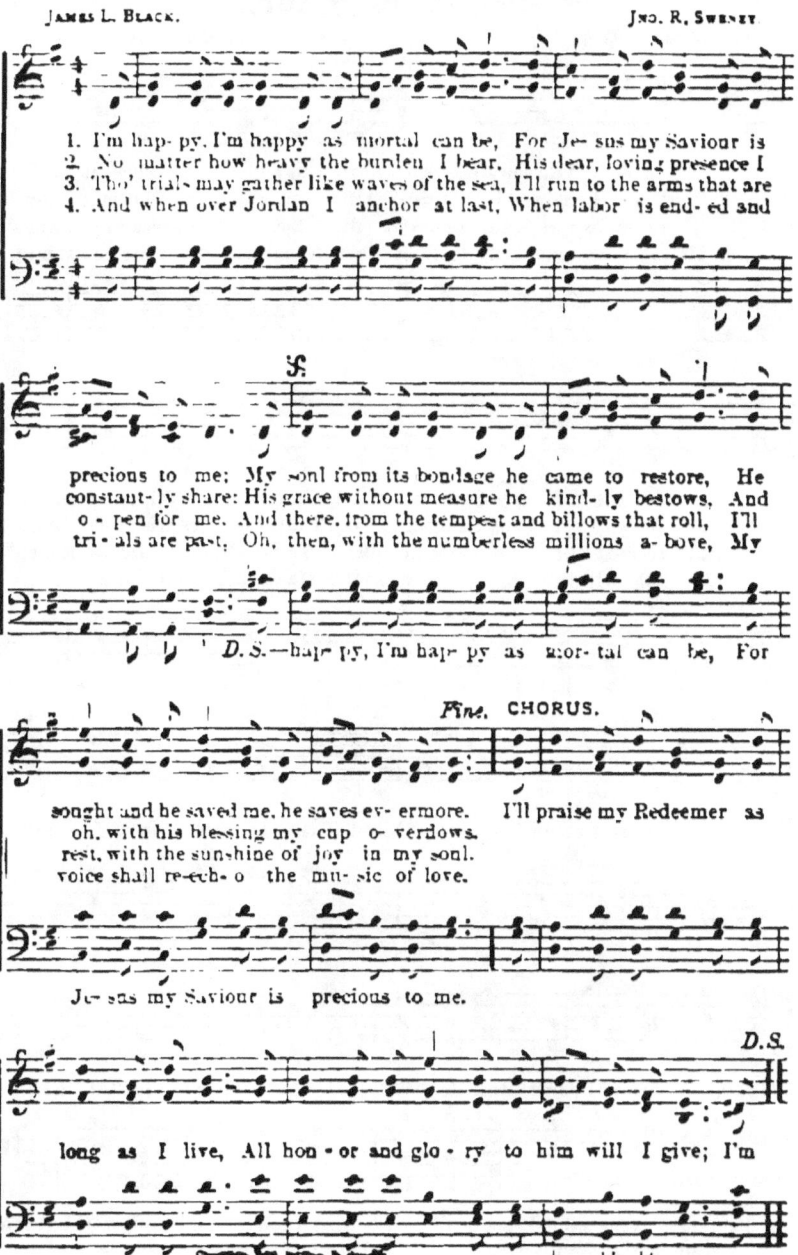

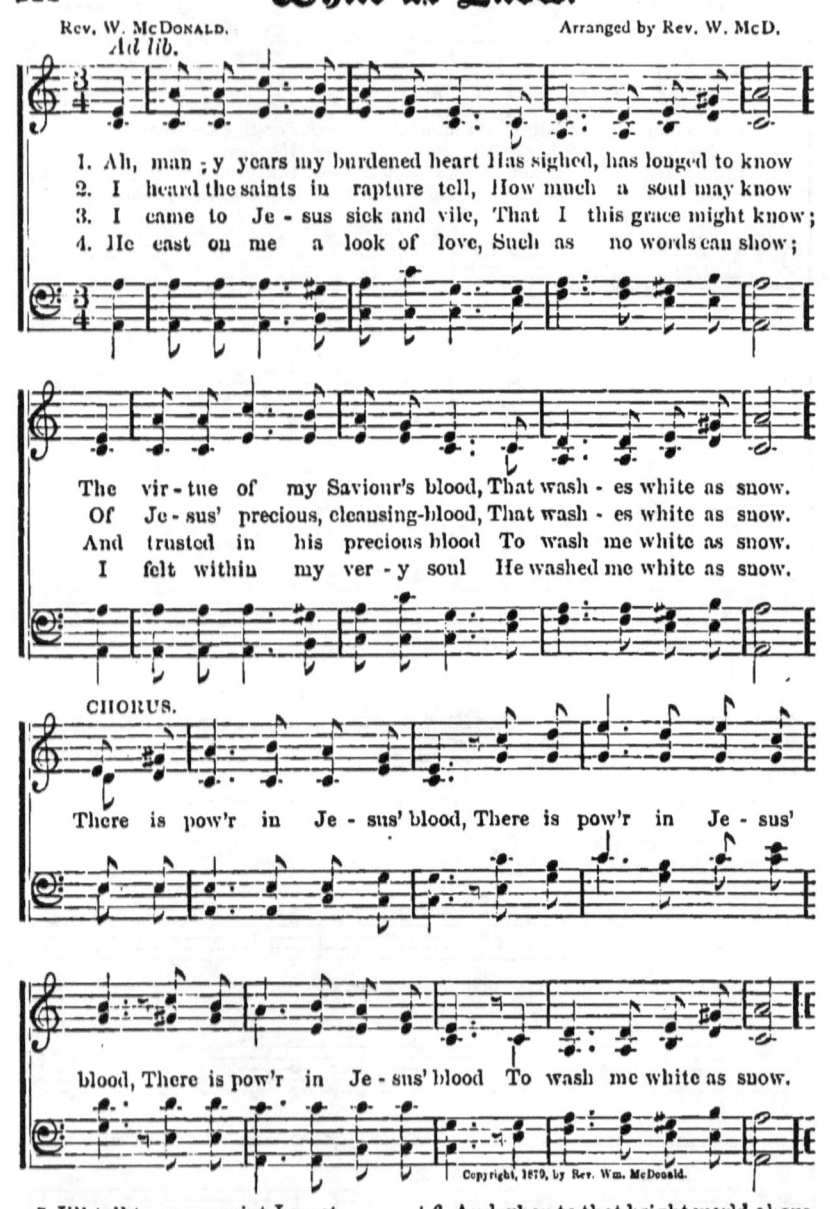

144. White as Snow.

Rev. W. McDonald. *Ad lib.* Arranged by Rev. W. McD.

1. Ah, man-y years my burdened heart Has sighed, has longed to know
   The vir-tue of my Saviour's blood, That wash-es white as snow.
2. I heard the saints in rapture tell, How much a soul may know
   Of Je-sus' precious, cleansing-blood, That wash-es white as snow.
3. I came to Je-sus sick and vile, That I this grace might know;
   And trusted in his precious blood To wash me white as snow.
4. He cast on me a look of love, Such as no words can show;
   I felt within my ver-y soul He washed me white as snow.

CHORUS.
There is pow'r in Je-sus' blood, There is pow'r in Je-sus' blood, There is pow'r in Je-sus' blood To wash me white as snow.

5. I'll tell to every saint I meet,
   To sinners high and low,
   That, trusting in the Saviour's blood,
   It washes white as snow.

6. And when to that bright world above
   My raptured soul shall go,
   My song shall be—the precious blood,
   Still washes white as snow.

He'll Mention Them no More. 145

"They shall not be mentioned unto him."—Ezek. xvii: 22.

E. E. Hewitt. Jno. R. Sweney.

1. My soul sings glory all the way, For Jesus took my sins away;
2. Oh, wondrous grace, so rich and free, That mentions not my sins to me,
3. But since he shows such grace to me, Let not his love forgotten be;
4. My soul sings glory all the way To yonder land of cloudless day,

With precious blood they're covered o'er, He'll mention them no more.
Since Jesus in redeeming love, Brought mercy from above.
Oh, let my life its tribute bring, My heart exultant sing.
And when I reach that happy shore, I'll praise him evermore.

CHORUS.

My sins . . . . . are all taken away, ... My
My sins are all taken away,

sins . . . are all taken away; . . . . . Oh, glory to his name!
sins are all taken away, My sins are all taken away;

Oh, glory to his name! My sins are all taken away, taken away.
taken away.

Praise in Song—K

Copyright, 1892, by Jno. R. Sweney.

The Sweet Beulah Land.

"Let us go up at once and possess it;" Nu. xiii: 30.

Rev. H. J. Zelley. H. L. Gilmour.

1. I am walking to-day in the sweet Beu-lah land, I have crossed to the glo-ry side, I am washed in the blood, and my soul is made white, And I know I am sanc-ti-fied.
2. I am now go-ing on to explore Beu-lah land, 'Tis the gift of my Lord to me; I am tasting its joys, I am walking in light, And the face of my Saviour see.
3. I have found a sweet peace that the world can-not know, As I walk by my Saviour's side, I am kept by his power, I am led by his hand, And I'll ev-er with him a-bide.
4. Oh, the sweetness of love that en-raptures my soul, For com-mun-ion with Christ I know! I am hap-py in him, and to-day thro' my soul Living streams of sal-va-tion flow.

CHORUS.

Glo-ry, Glo-ry to God, My heart is now cleansed from sin, . I've abandoned my-self to the Ho-ly Ghost, And his ful-ness a-bides with-in.

Glory to God, oh, from sin,

Copyright, 1891, by H. L. Gilmour.

Who will Follow Jesus? 147

F. E. Hewitt.
Wm. J. Kirkpatrick.

1. Who will follow Je-sus, Standing for the right, Holding up his banner
2. Who will follow Je-sus In life's busy ways, Working for the Master,
3. Who will follow Jesus? When the tempter charms, Fleeing then, for safety
4. Who will follow Je-sus In his work of love? Leading others to him,

In the thickest fight? List'ning for his or-ders, Read-y to o-bey,
Giving him the praise? Earnest in his vineyard, Hon-or-ing his laws,
To the Saviour's arms; Trusting in his mer-cy, Trusting in his power,
Lifting prayers above; Courage, faithful servant; In his word we see,

CHORUS.

Who will follow Je-sus, Serving him to-day? Who will follow Je-sus?
Faithful to his counsel, Watchful for his cause?
Seeking fresh renewals Of his grace each hour.
On our side forev-er Will this Saviour be.

Who will make reply, "I am on the Lord's side, Master, here am I?" Who will follow

Je-sus? Who will make reply, "I am on the Lord's side, Master, here am I?"

Copyright, 1892, by Wm. J. Kirkpatrick.

148. The Good Ship Zion.

L. H. Edmunds.   Wm. J. Kirkpatrick.

1. O come, O come! for staunch and strong, The good ship Zion sails along; O come and join her happy crew, And trust the Captain wise and true. We bear his banner floating from the mast, And hope thro' grace to reach our home at last; Then join with our number; we're bound to the land of light; We'll keep our course onward thro' the stormy night.

2. Our chart will show when rocks are near, The polar-star is shining clear; When billows seem to overwhelm We'll trust the Hand that holds the helm. Then lift on high the banner of the cross, The ship that bears it never suffers loss; Obeying his orders, tho' gales of temptation come, The Captain of salvation surely guides us home.

3. Beyond life's tossing, fitful sea, The haven lies where we would be, And soon, with rays of glory bright, We'll hail the beacon's welcome light. The good ship Zion, tho' the breakers roar, Will safely land us on the morning shore; Then over the surges we sail to the port of peace, With joy we'll cast the anchor when the voyage shall cease.

CHORUS.

Sailing, sailing over the sea of time,

Copyright, 1893, by Wm. J. Kirkpatrick.

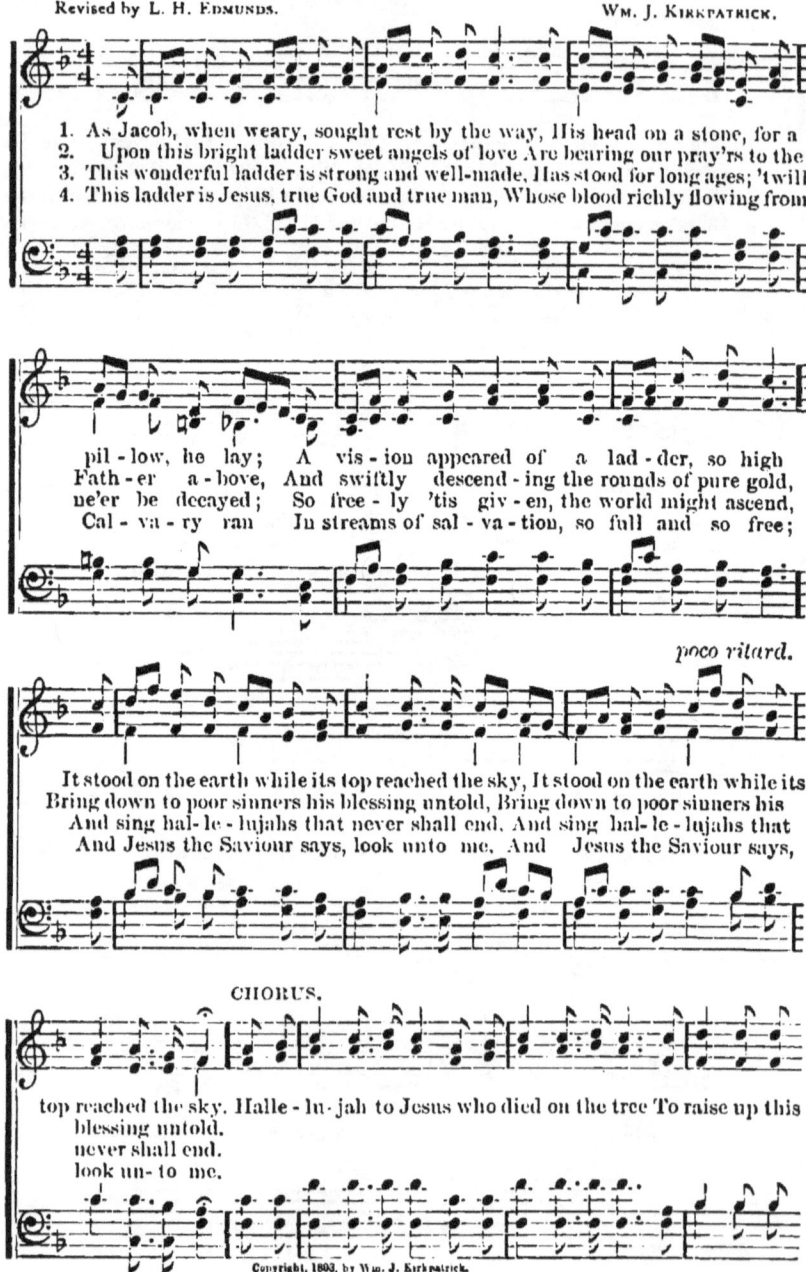

The Ladder of Mercy.—CONCLUDED.

5 Our fathers upon it have mounted to God,
  They've finished their labors, and reached their abode,
  And we're climbing after, and soon we'll be there,
  To join with the ransomed, their happiness share.

6 We'll see our dear Saviour, and join the glad throng
  In singing his praises in rapturous song;
  All glory to God, to the Father and Son,
  And blest Holy Spirit, united in one.

Go as an Humble Disciple.

MARY THOMPSON. JNO. R. SWENEY.

1. Go as an humble dis-ci-ple, Pray'rfully, earnestly go;
2. Go to the poor and neglect-ed, Seek them where'er they may be;
3. Rescue the lost ones that per-ish, Urge them at once to be-lieve,
4. Go with a word from the Master, Go with his love in thy heart;

Whisper the name of the Sav-iour Tender-ly, soft-ly and low.
Tell them the sto-ry of Je-sus, Tell them his mercy is free.
Some one will list to thy pleading, Some one the truth will re-ceive.
Scatter its sunshine of glad-ness, Bidding the shadows de-part.

D.S.—Follow his blessed ex-am-ple, He will thy la-bor re-ward.

CHORUS.

Go as an humble dis-ci-ple, Go for the sake of thy Lord;

Copyright, 1893, by Jno. R. Sweney.

156. A Sunny Side of Life.

A. ROSALTHE CAREY.
WM. J. KIRKPATRICK.

1. Oh, sigh not in sorrow for the joys that will not stay, Nor dim all the present with the thought of coming ill; Let no cloud of to-morrow shade the brightness of to-day, For each cloud has its bow of promise still.
2. Though trial and toil have found a home in ev'ry land, And care, like a phantom, haunts each earthly gleam of light; Yet, the angel of faith will point her snowy, gentle hand, To the realms where will come no grief nor night.
3. Each heart has its burden and its weary, weary pain, And tears oft will gather on the smile of love and hope; But, the tears of his children God will change to smiles again, And pour balm in their ev'ry bit-ter cup.

Copyright, 1893, by Wm. J. Kirkpatrick.

A Sunny Side of Life.—CONCLUDED. 157

Then look where the bright sun is shining, O'er the shadows of this weary world of [strife,
Then look, look where the bright sun is shining, ... world, this weary world of strife,

For each cloud has its fair, silver lining, Praise God! there's a sunny side of life.
For each cloud has its fair, has its fair, silver lining, side, a sunny side of life.

My only Intercessor.

F. G. Burroughs.   Isa. lix: 16.   H. L. Gilmour.

1. Though numbered with the sin-defiled, I am my Father's long-sought child;
2. In naught but filthy rags I come, Yet, weary of these paths I roam,
3. No more, among the husks and swine, With want and hunger I repine;
4. Though coming empty to thy feet, My soul with joy is made replete;

And now my soul is reconciled, O Lamb of God, through thee!
I seek at last my Father's home, O Lamb of God, through thee!
The ring, the robe, the kiss are mine, O Lamb of God, through thee!
Mine is the Father's pardon sweet, O Lamb of God, through thee!

D. S.—my behalf points to his side, My on-ly In-ter - - cessor.

CHORUS.   D.S.

The Lamb of God, who for me died, And on the cross was crucified, In

Copyright, 1883, by H. L. Gilmour.

Resting 'Neath His Shadow.

Rev. H. J. Zelley. Jno. R. Sweney.

1. There's no comfort in the pleasures of the earth, In its ma-ny follies,
2. If the clouds of darkness shall surround my way, I will trust in him who
3. When my foes oppress me, and my friends forsake, I will look to Je-sus
4. Soon my warfare end-ed and my tri-als past, I will join the rapturous

and its senseless mirth; I will live for Je-sus, walking in his light,
changes night to day; And a-mid life's conflicts, while I do the right,
and fresh courage take; In a world of sorrow, strengthened by his might,
song of "heaven at last;" As I stand before him faith will change to sight,

D.S.—liv-ing where the sky is ev-er bright,

Fine. CHORUS.

I will rest beneath his shadow with delight. I am rest-ing in the
I can sit beneath his shadow with delight.
I can sit beneath his shadow with delight.
And I'll gaze upon his beauty with delight.

I am sitting 'neath his shadow with delight.

D.S.

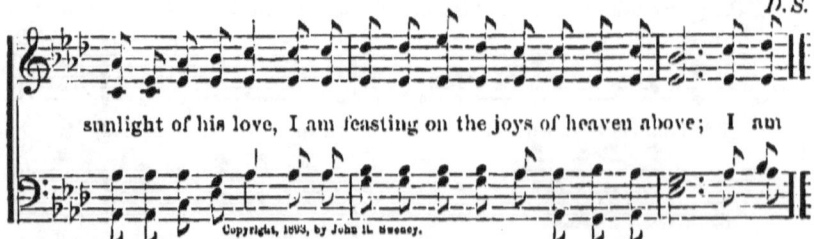

sunlight of his love, I am feasting on the joys of heaven above; I am

Copyright, 1893, by John R. Sweney.

Blessed Refuge.

159

FANNY J. CROSBY.
Mrs. Rev. J. G. WILSON.

ALTO OR BASS SOLO.

1. Blessed refuge of the soul, With thy love o'ershadow me;
2. Blessed refuge, mine a-lone, While in fervent pray'r I bend;
3. Blessed refuge, ev-er near, Precious balm for all my woes;

CHO.—Blessed refuge of the soul, With thy love o'ershadow me;

Fine.

Still the raging waves con-trol, Keep my anchor firm on thee.
From thy bright ce-les-tial throne Let the star of faith descend,
What have I to ask or fear While I still on thee re-pose?

Still the raging waves con-trol, Keep my anchor firm on thee.

Gent-ly o'er the ocean's foam Cheer my heart and guide my way;
May its pure and sacred rays, Breaking thro' the clouds of night,
Soon with angels I shall rise Far above this changeful shore,

D. C. Chorus.

Till I hear thy welcome home, Safe within the gates of day.
Fill my waking thoughts with praise, Till I hail the morning light.
Where the dawning never dies, And tho darkness comes no more.

Copyright, 1880, by Jno. R. Sweney.

I Glory in the Cross.—CONCLUDED

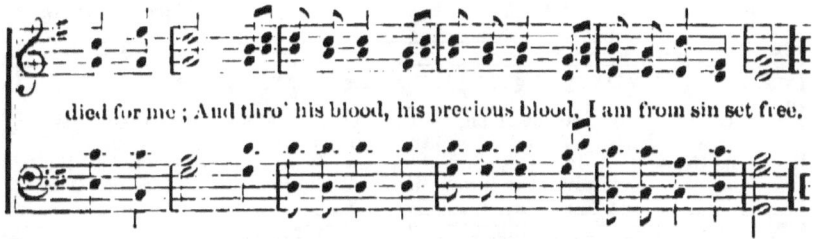

died for me; And thro' his blood, his precious blood, I am from sin set free.

I will Praise Him.

L. H. EDMUNDS. JNO. R. SWENEY.

1. Sing with me in joy-ful measure, Sing my dear Redeemer's love;
2. To his precious cross I'm clinging, Plunging in the cleansing tide,
3. Sweeter grows salvation's sto-ry, As I learn its meaning more;
4. Blessed bells of promise pealing, Onward call the willing soul;
5. I will praise him, I will praise him, Pressing on life's varied way;

Sing the rich, e-ter-nal treasures Je-sus brings me from a-bove.
There he fills my lips with singing. There my needs are all supplied.
Christ within, "the hope of glo-ry," Op'ning Heav-en's roy-al store.
Mighty grace his word re-vealing, Let the hal-le-lu-jahs roll.
I will praise him, I will praise him, Where his smile is endless day

D. S.—rise from earth to heaven, I will shout his praise on high.

CHORUS. D.S.

I will praise him, I will praise him, I will praise him till I die; When I

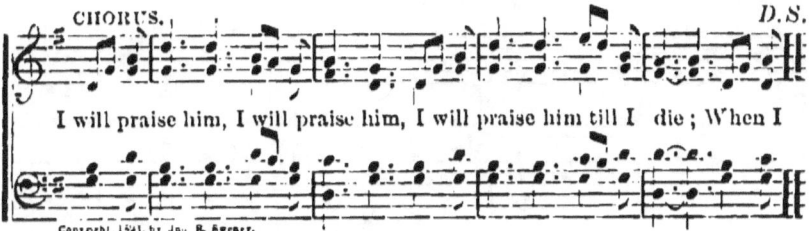

Copyright, 1893, by Jno. R. Sweney.

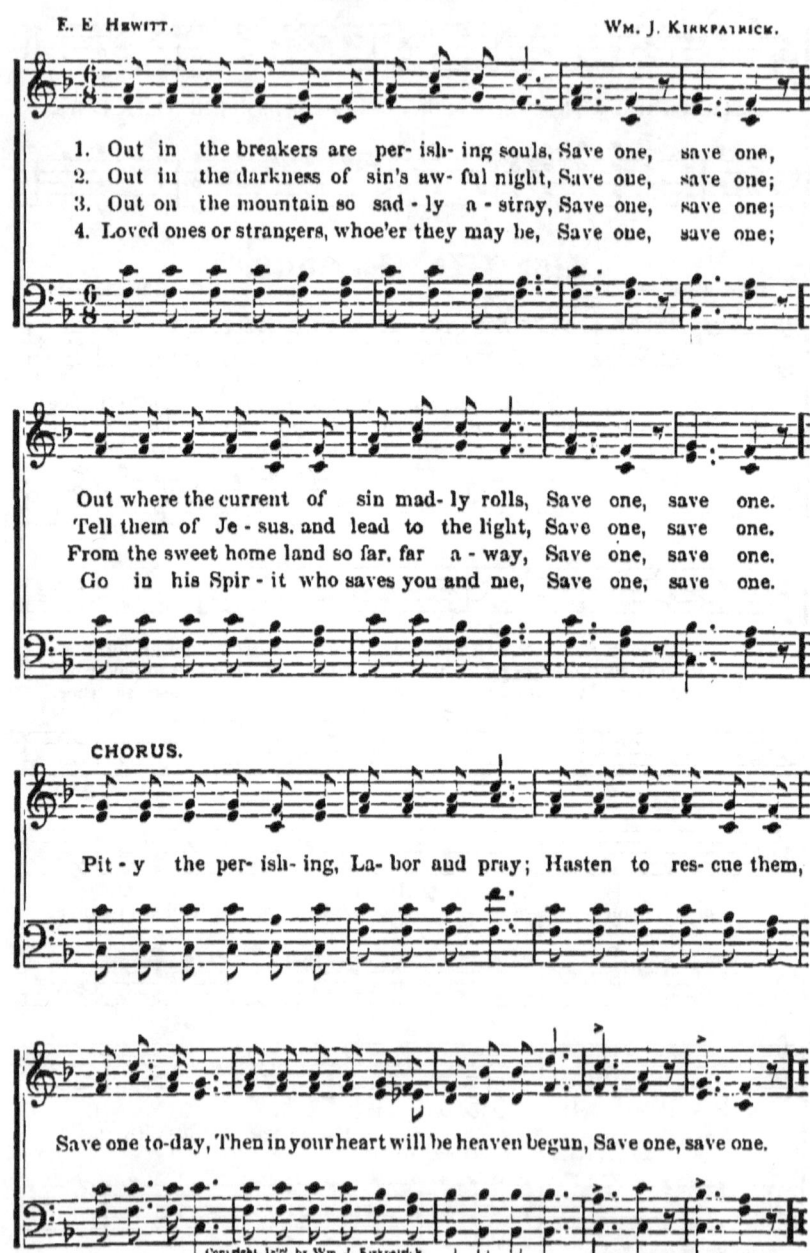

I Now Believe. 173

Isaac Watts.   Wm. J. Kirkpatrick.

1. A-las! and did my Saviour bleed? And did my Sovereign die?
2. Was it for crimes that I have done, He groaned upon the tree?
3. Well might the sun in darkness hide, And shut his glories in,
4. Thus might I hide my blushing face, While his dear cross appears;
5. But drops of grief can ne'er re-pay The debt of love I owe:

Would he devote that sacred head For such a worm as I?
A-mazing pity! grace unknown! And love beyond degree!
When Christ, the mighty Maker, died For man, the creature's sin.
Dis-solve my heart in thankfulness, And melt mine eyes to tears.
Here, Lord, I give my-self away,—'Tis all that I can do.

CHORUS.

I now be-lieve he died for me. I now believe, I now believe;
Oh, wondrous grace, so full and free, I now believe he died for me.

Copyright, 1886, by Wm. J. Kirkpatrick.

Why Not To-Day?

Wm. H. Gardner.
Frank M. Davis.

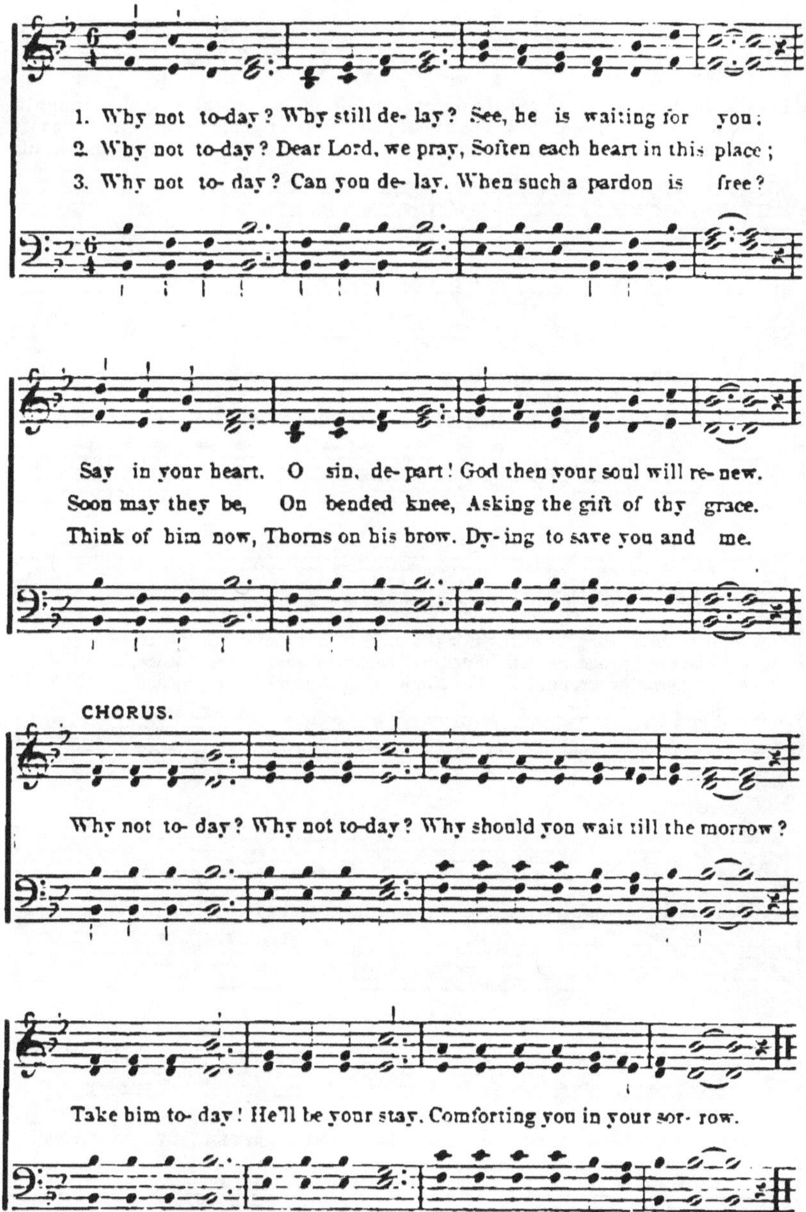

1. Why not to-day? Why still de-lay? See, he is waiting for you;
2. Why not to-day? Dear Lord, we pray, Soften each heart in this place;
3. Why not to-day? Can you de-lay, When such a pardon is free?

Say in your heart, O sin, de-part! God then your soul will re-new.
Soon may they be, On bended knee, Asking the gift of thy grace.
Think of him now, Thorns on his brow, Dy-ing to save you and me.

CHORUS.

Why not to-day? Why not to-day? Why should you wait till the morrow?

Take him to-day! He'll be your stay, Comforting you in your sor-row.

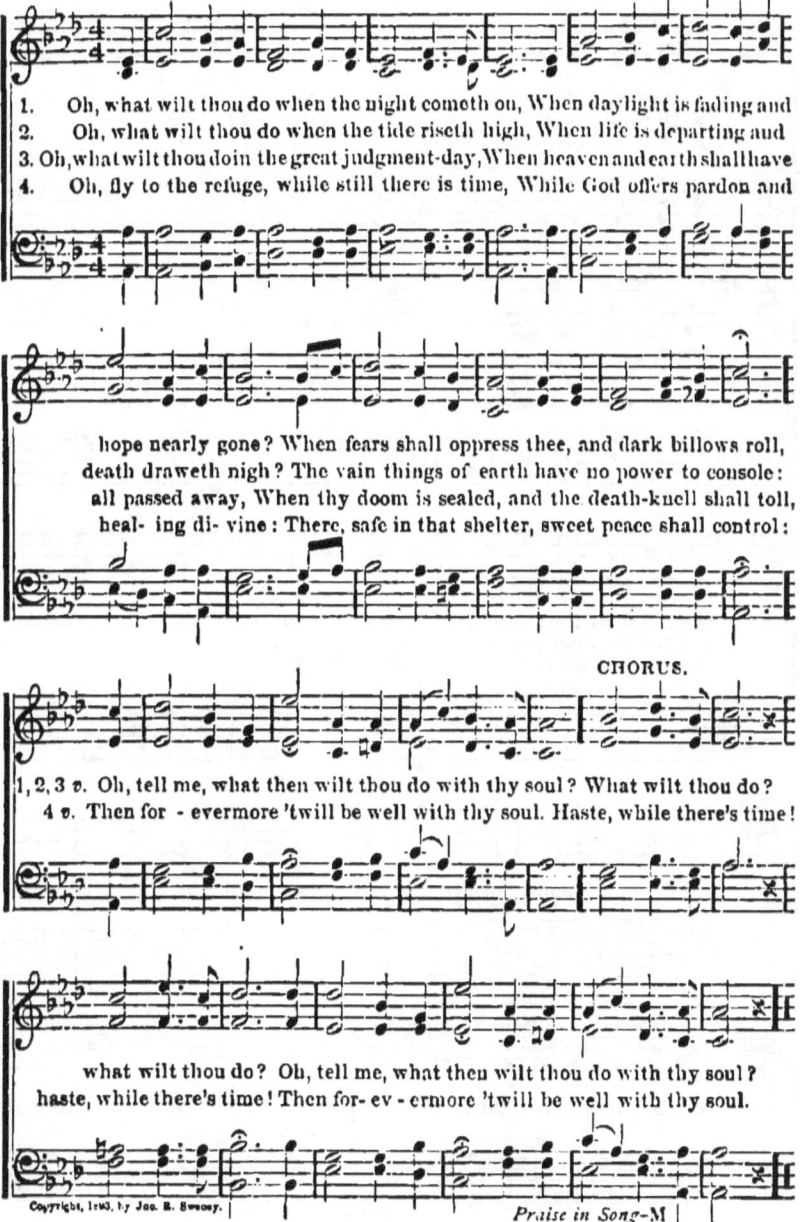

Keep Close to Jesus.

179

J. L.   JOHN LANE.

1. When you start for the land of heaven-ly rest, Keep close to
2. Nev-er mind the storms or tri-als as you go, Keep close to
3. To be safe from the darts of the e-vil one, Keep close to
4. We shall reach our home in heaven by and bye, Keep close to

Jesus all the way; For he is the Guide, and he knows the way best,
Jesus all the way; 'Tis a comfort and joy his fa-vor to know,
Jesus all the way; Take the shield of faith till the vic-to-ry is won,
Jesus all the way; Where to those we love we'll never say good-bye,

CHORUS.

Keep close to Je-sus all the way. Keep close to Je-sus, Keep close to Je-sus, Keep close to Je-sus all the way; By day or by night never turn from the right, Keep close to Jesus all the way.

Copyright, 1872, 1878, by John J. Hood.

The Saviour Found Me.

Thos. E. Roach.   H. L. Gilmour.

1. I was a wayward, wand'ring child, I walked in sin, I was defiled,
2. I turned and sought forgiving grace, My Saviour showed his lovely face,
3. No carping cares depress me now, No fear of ill disturbs my brow,
4. Adieu to sin and vain desire! My soul has caught the heav'nly fire,

Oh, how the world my soul beguiled! How dark the night around me!
I felt his blood my sins ef-face, He saved me, hal-le-lu-jah!
No storms affright, tho' loud they blow, Since Jesus is my Sav-iour.
And now, with joy, my pow'rs aspire Toward heav'n, my home in glo-ry.

But, while I wandered far a-way, I heard the voice of Je-sus say:—
My load of sin then rolled a-way, My night was sweetly turned to day,
Content-ed in his love I rest, I go or stay at his behest;
Come on, my friends, companions, come, No more in sin an ex-ile roam;

S.   *Fine.*

"Come, fol-low me, I am the way;" Oh, yes! the Saviour found me.
My feet are in the nar-row way, I've found the land of Beu-lah.
My days glide on, su-premely blest, While walking in his fa-vor.
The price is paid, who will may come, Oh, wondrous, wondrous sto-ry!

D. S.—I'll tell the sto-ry where I go, That Je-sus is my Sav-iour.

CHORUS.   *D. S.*

Oh, he's my Sav-iour, this I know, For he the wit-ness doth bestow;

Copyright, 1893, by H. L. Gilmour.

184. Stop, Sinner, Stop.

J. B. Mackay.
Mrs. Rev. J. G. Wilson.

1. Stop, sinner, stop, you have wandered astray, Some e-vil lies hidden each step of your way; Where others have perished you thoughtlessly tread, Don't follow that pathway, there's danger ahead.
2. Stop, sinner, stop, take a moment to think, The chasm is yawning, you're nearing its brink; Oh, think of the loved ones, whose hearts for you yearn, They're watching and praying for you to return.
3. Stop, sinner, stop in your downward career, Its end is destruction, oh, why per-severe? The Saviour is call-ing, how can you de-lay? In mercy he warns you, oh, heed him to-day.
4. Stop, sinner, stop, turn to Je-sus and live, The master you're serving no respite will give; There's safety in turn-ing, oh, why do you wait? To-morrow it may be for-ev-er too late.

CHORUS.

Stop, sinner, stop, turn back or be lost, The gulf just before you can never be crossed; Your soul is in danger, oh, sin-ner, beware, Turn back, leave the pathway of sin and despair.

Copyright, 1888, by Jno. R. Sweney.

Where is Thy Soul?

MARTHA J. LANKTON.   WM. J. KIRKPATRICK.

1. Oft hast thou heard a voice that said, In tones that were soft and low,
2. Oft hast thou heard a warning voice, That urged thee to fly from sin,
3. Oft hast thou heard a tender voice, When troubled and care-oppressed,
4. Oft hast thou heard a grieved, sad voice, Entreating thee o'er and o'er;

Thy Saviour has loved and loves thee yet, Then why wilt thou slight him so?
To open the door you long have closed, And welcome the Saviour in.
And then, like a weary child, hast sighed In Jesus to find a rest.
And if thou refuse to hear it now, Perhaps it will come no more.

CHORUS.

Where is thy soul? where is thy soul? Where is thy soul to-night?
4th v.—Yield to him now, yield to him now, Give him thy soul to-night;

That voice pleads on, pleads patiently on, Oh, where is thy soul to-night?
That voice pleads on, pleads patiently on, Oh, give him thy soul to-night.

Copyright, 1886, 1889, by Wm. J. Kirkpatrick

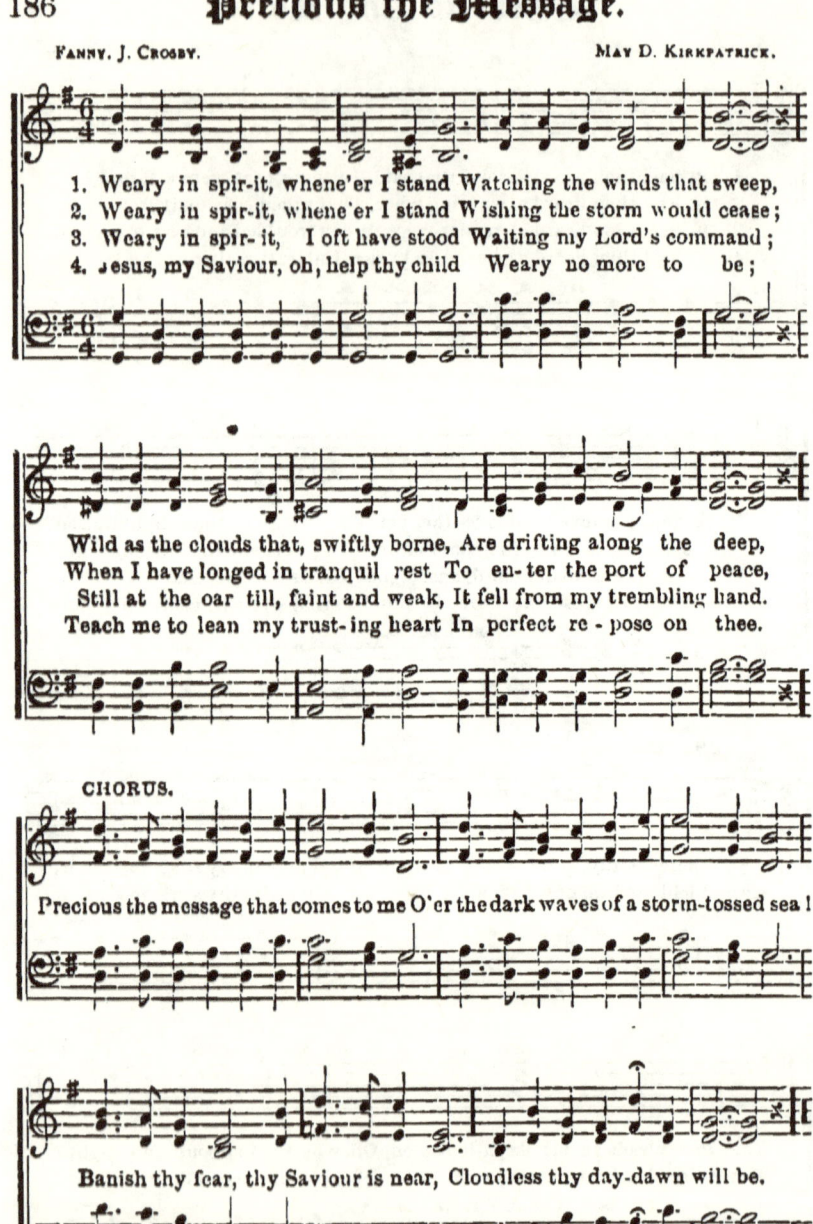

Jesus Leads.

187

"And when he putteth forth his own sheep, he goeth before them, and the sheep follow him; for they know his voice."—John x: 4.

John R. Clements. Jno. R. Sweney.

Andante.

1. Like a shepherd, tender, true, Jesus leads, ... Jesus leads, ..
   Daily finds us pastures new, Jesus leads, ... Jesus leads; ..
   If thick mists are o'er the way, ... Or the flock 'mid danger feeds, ..
   He will watch them lest they stray, Jesus leads, .. Jesus leads.

2. All along life's rugged road Jesus leads, ... Jesus leads, ..
   Till we reach yon blest abode, Jesus leads, ... Jesus leads; ..
   All the way, before, he's trod, And he now the flock precedes, ..
   Safe into the fold of God Jesus leads, .. Jesus leads.

3. Thro' the sun-lit ways of life Jesus leads, ... Jesus leads, ..
   Thro' the warings and the strife Jesus leads, ... Jesus leads; ..
   When we reach the Jordan's tide, Where life's bound'ry-line recedes, ..
   He will spread the waves aside, Jesus leads, .. Jesus leads.

Copyright, 1893, by Jno. R. Sweney.

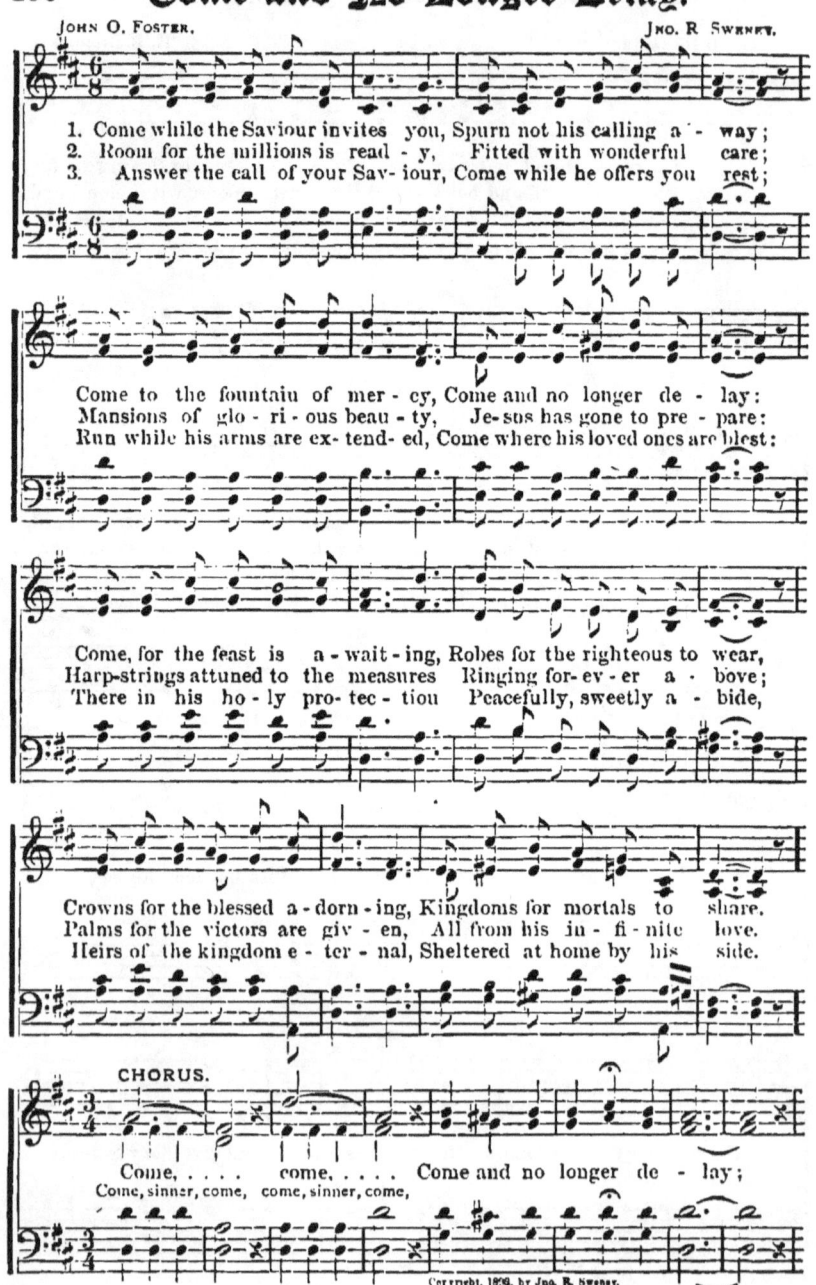

Come and No Longer, etc.—CONCLUDED.

Come while the Saviour invites you, Come and no longer de-lay....
no longer delay.

Living in Canaan.

H. L. GILMOUR.   Num. xiii : 30.   H. RUSSELL.
Adapt. and arr. by H. L. G.

1. Let us go and possess the land, Old faith-ful Ca-leb cried, We're
2. I'm living where clusters hang, By Eschol's sun-lit rills, Where
3. How blessed as I ex-plore The land I have pos-sessed, And
4. And still there's another land, Where temptation cometh not, Where

CHO.—I'm o-ver in Canaan now, The crossing was made by faith; I'm

Fine.

able to o'ercome; The Lord is on our side, We fear no giants great, Nor
corn and wine with oil And honey sweet distills, No yoke of bondage dread, For
reach another peak Of trusting, constant rest; I'm walking thro' the Land Where
foes and wall'd defence Are evermore forgot; But where the conq'ror's song, Floats

trusting Jesus' blood, His arms are underneath.

D. C. Chorus.

grim old walls affright, The order "go" inspires us so, They'll fall before we fight.
ev'ry chain is riv'n, Christ gives his easy yoke instead, And makes us heirs of heav'n.
Jesus safely leads, In pastures green he's always seen, And hidden manna feeds.
out o'er all the plains, And seraph's anthems ever blend With alleluia strains.

Copyright, 1893, by H. L. Gilmour.

193. Our Loving Friend.

FANNY J. CROSBY.   C. M. Double.   WM. J. KIRKPATRICK.

1. There is a bond of u-nion sweet, Not death it-self can break,
2. There is a song of joy be-yond, And o'er a waveless stream,
3. There is a time, there is a place, Where toil and strife shall cease,

For he who formed its sa-cred links His own will ne'er for-sake;
It comes to us on ser-aph wings, Like mu-sic in a dream;
Where rest-less wind and storm-y wave Shall all be hushed to peace;

There is a Friend, a loving Friend, Who knows our ev-'ry care,
It comes from him, our loving Friend, Whose name we breathe in prayer,
And we shall see our loving Friend, And sing his triumph there,

Who bore the cross, with all its pain, That we the crown might wear.

Copyright, 1893, by Wm. J. Kirkpatrick.

194.   On Jordan's stormy Banks I stand.   *Tune above.*

On Jordan's stormy banks I stand,
  And cast a wishful eye
To Canaan's fair and happy land,
  Where my possessions lie.
O the transporting, rapturous scene
  That rises to my sight!
Sweet fields arrayed in living green,
  And rivers of delight.

2 O'er all these wide-extended plains
  Shines one eternal day;
There God the Son forever reigns,
  And scatters night away.

No chilling winds, or poisonous breath,
  Can reach that healthful shore;
Sickness and sorrow, pain and death,
  Are felt and feared no more.

3 When shall I reach that happy place,
  And be forever blest?
When shall I see my Father's face,
  And in his bosom rest?
Filled with delight, my raptured soul
  Would here no longer stay:
Though Jordan's waves around me roll,
  Fearless I'd launch away.

Praise in Song–N

195 Living Like Christ.

E. E. H., suggested by Rev. C. Roads.
Wm. J. Kirkpatrick.

1. Liv-ing to save the lost, Liv-ing like Christ; Helping the tempest-toss'd, Liv-ing like Christ. Oh, may his grace be mine, His love within me shine, Strengthened by power divine, Living like Christ.
2. Be this my blessed aim, Liv-ing like Christ; Bearing his precious name, Liv-ing like Christ; Counting the world but dross, All other gain but loss, Taking the hallowed cross, Living like Christ.
3. Liv-ing, his face to see, Liv-ing like Christ; Pure, like him-self to be, Liv-ing like Christ. Wearing his robe of white, Walk-ing the way of light, Till faith is ful-ly sight, Liv-ing like Christ.

Copyright, 1893, by Wm. J. Kirkpatrick.

196 I Love Thee. 11s.

Arranged by W. J. K.

1. I love thee, I love thee, I love thee, my Lord; I love thee, my
2. I'm hap-py, I'm hap-py, oh, wondrous account! My joys are im-
3. O Je-sus, my Saviour! with thee I am blest! My life and sal-
4. Oh, who's like my Saviour! he's Salem's bright King! He smiles, and he

198. Step Out on the Promise.

MAGGIE POTTER. Arr. by E. F. M.   E. F. MILLER.

1. O mourner in Zi-on, how blessed art thou, For Je-sus is waiting to com-fort thee now, Fear not to re-ly on the word of thy God; Step out on the promise,—get under the blood.
2. O ye that are hun-gry and thirsty, re-joice! For ye shall be filled; do you hear that sweet voice In-vit-ing you now to the ban-quet of God? Step out on the promise,—get under the blood.
3. Who sighs for a heart from in-i-qui-ty free? O poor, troubled soul! there's a promise for thee, There's rest, weary one, in the bos-om of God; Step out on the promise,—get under the blood.
4. Step out on the promise, and Christ you shall win, "The blood of his Son cleanseth us from all sin," It cleanseth me now, hal-le-lu-jah to God! I rest on his promise,—I'm under the blood.

From "The Shout of Victory," by per

199. Bless the Lord, my Soul.

E. A. BARNES.   WM. J. KIRKPATRICK.

1. Oh, bless the Lord, my soul, As the friend who died for thee; And bless him
2. Oh, bless the Lord, my soul, As the rock in which we hide; And bless him
3. Oh, bless the Lord, my soul, As the hope so sure and sweet; And bless him
4. Oh, bless the Lord, my soul, As the guide in days to come; And bless him

Copyright, 1893, by Wm. J. Kirkpatrick.

201. In the Lord is our Hope.

MARTHA J. LANKTON. WM. J. KIRKPATRICK.

1. In the Lord is our hope, On his word we are stayed, With its truth our defense We shall not be dismayed.
2. In the Lord is our trust, And his name we adore, For his kingdom shall stand When the world is no more.
3. In the Lord is our strength, And we dread not our foes; We shall conquer thro' grace, Though a host may oppose.
4. In the Lord is our rest; Oh, the joy we shall see When his welcome we hear, And from toil we are free.

CHORUS.

Hal-le-lu-jah! hal-le-lu-jah! Oh, exalt him again! Hal-le-lu-jah in the highest, Halle-lu-jah, a-men.

Copyright, 1896, by Wm. J. Kirkpatrick.

202. Choose the Saviour.

"Choose you this day whom ye will serve."—Josh. xxiv: 17.

H. L. G. H. L. GILMOUR.

1. Come to Jesus, wand'rer, come, Still he waits to welcome home;
2. Come to Jesus as you are, Break from Satan's ev-'ry snare,
3. Come to Jesus, why decline Love's fond pleadings, heart of thine?
4. Come to Jesus, now re-lent, Come, be-liev-ing-ly re-pent;
*5. Hal-le-lu-jah, Jesus saves! Sing it loud, ye ransomed slaves;

Copyright, 1890, by H. L. Gilmour.

* If sung as a Solo the 5th verse to be sung by Choir and Congregation.

204. Watchman, Tell us of the Night.

Sir John Bowring.   Tune, WATCHMAN. 7s, d.

1. Watchman, tell us of the night, What its signs of promise are;
   Traveler, o'er yon mountain's height See that glo-ry-beaming star!
   Watchman, does its beauteous ray Aught of hope or joy fore-tell?
   Traveler, yes; it brings the day, Promised day of Is-ra-el.
2. Watchman, tell us of the night; Higher yet that star ascends.
   Traveler, bless-edness and light, Peace and truth its course portends!
   Watchman, will its beams a-lone Gild the spot that gave them birth?
   Traveler, a-ges are its own, See, it bursts o'er all the earth!
3. Watchman, tell us of the night, For the morning seems to dawn;
   Traveler, darkness takes its flight; Doubt and ter-ror are withdrawn.
   Watchman, let thy wandering cease; Hie thee to thy qui-et home!
   Traveler, lo! the Prince of Peace, Lo! the Son of God is come!

205.   Jesus, Lover of My Soul.   *Tune above.*

Jesus, Lover of my soul,
  Let me to thy bosom fly,
While the nearer waters roll,
  While the tempest still is high!
Hide me, O my Saviour, hide,
  Till the storm of life is past;
Safe into the haven guide,
  O receive my soul at last!

2 Other refuge have I none;
  Hangs my helpless soul on thee:
Leave, oh, leave me not alone,
  Still support and comfort me:
All my trust on thee is stayed,
  All my help from thee I bring;
Cover my defenceless head
  With the shadow of thy wing!

3 Plenteous grace with thee is found
  Grace to cover all my sin:
Let the healing streams abound:
  Make and keep me pure within.
Thou of life the fountain art,
  Freely let me take of thee.
Spring thou up within my heart,
  Rise to all eternity.

Creation. L. M. D.

FRANCIS JOSEPH HAYDN.

206 The heavens declare his glory.

1 THE spacious firmament on high,
  With all the blue ethereal sky,
And spangled heavens, a shining frame,
  Their great Original proclaim:
The unwearied sun, from day to day,
  Doth his Creator's power display,
And publishes to every land
  The work of an almighty hand.

2 Soon as the evening shades prevail,
  The moon takes up the wondrous tale,
And nightly, to the listening earth,
  Repeats the story of her birth;
While all the stars that round her burn,
  And all the planets in their turn,
Confirm the tidings as they roll,
  And spread the truth from pole to pole.

3 What though in solemn silence all
  Move round the dark terrestrial ball?
What though no real voice nor sound
  Amid the radiant orbs be found?
In reason's ear they all rejoice,
  And utter forth a glorious voice;
Forever singing as they shine,
  "The hand that made us is divine."

JOSEPH ADDISON.

207 Jehovah's sovereignty.

1 FATHER of all, whose powerful voice
  Called forth this universal frame!
Whose mercies over all rejoice,
  Through endless ages still the same;
Thou by thy word upholdest all;
  Thy bounteous love to all is showed;
Thou hear'st thy every creature's call,
  And fillest every mouth with good.

2 In heaven thou reign'st enthroned in light,
  Nature's expanse before thee spread;
Earth, air, and sea, before thy sight,
  And hell's deep gloom, are open laid;
Wisdom, and might, and love are thine;
  Prostrate before thy face we fall,
Confess thine attributes divine,
  And hail thee sovereign Lord of all.

3 Blessings and honor, praise and love,
  Co-equal, co-eternal Three,
In earth below, in heaven above,
  By all thy works, be paid to thee.
Let all who owe to thee their birth,
  In praises every hour employ;
Jehovah reigns! be glad, O earth,
  And shout, ye morning stars, for joy!

JOHN WESLEY.

208. When we all Get Home.

FANNY J. CROSBY.   JNO. R. SWENEY.

1. When we all get home, oh, happy, happy day! And our sorrows here are past;
2. When the morn shall break, oh, happy, happy morn! When its glories fill the skies,
3. When we all get home, oh, welcome, welcome hour! When the promis'd crown is won
4. Let us watch and pray, and journey, journey on, All our burdens meekly bear,

When we cross the sea, the narrow, narrow sea, And are gathered safe at last.
When we meet to rest for-ev-er, ever more, What a shout of joy will rise.
We shall hear a voice, a gentle, gentle voice, That will say to us well done.
Till we reach the land, the sunny, sunny land, Where the many mansions are.

D.S.—song we'll sing our blessed, blessed King, Sing it on the golden shore.

CHORUS.

When we all get home, o'er the billow's foam, And the weary night is o'er, What a

Copyright, 1893, by Jno. R. Sweney.

209. Saviour, take Me now.

HETTIE I. WILDE.   WM. J. KIRKPATRICK.

1. Saviour, hear my pleading, All thy mercy needing, To thy pastures leading,
2. Where the fount is flowing,   Where bright beams are glowing,
                  Life and peace bestowing,
3. Let thy peace enfold me, And thy arms uphold me, Half has not been told me,
4. When my heart grows weary, 'Mid the shadows dreary, Let thy comfort cheer me,
5. When my earthly story Lies complete before thee, To thy home of glory,

Copyright, 1893, by Wm. J. Kirkpatrick.

Do what You Can, etc.—CONCLUDED.

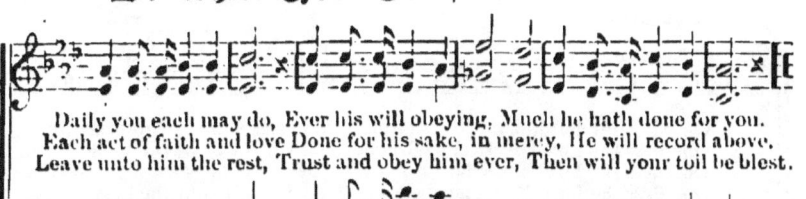

Daily you each may do, Ever his will obeying, Much he hath done for you.
Each act of faith and love Done for his sake, in mercy, He will record above.
Leave unto him the rest, Trust and obey him ever, Then will your toil be blest.

213 Within thy Courts, O Lord.

E. A. BARNES. WM. J. KIRKPATRICK.

1. Within thy courts, O Lord, We come again to-day; We come to meet thy
2. Within thy courts, O Lord, Unite our hearts to thee; And manifest thy
3. Within thy courts, O Lord, We worship at thy feet; And may we all be

CHO.—Within thy courts, O Lord, 'Tis sweet to praise and pray; Within thy courts, O

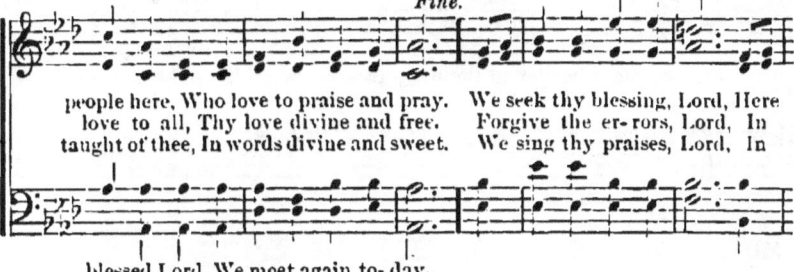

people here, Who love to praise and pray.   We seek thy blessing, Lord, Here
love to all, Thy love divine and free.   Forgive the er-rors, Lord, In
taught of thee, In words divine and sweet.   We sing thy praises, Lord, In

blessed Lord, We meet again to-day.

D. C. Chorus.

in this holy place; We ask of thee, for one and all, Renewals of thy grace.
which we often fall; And may the spirit of thy grace Abide with one and all.
notes of joy and love; And may we come to praise again, In higher courts above.

Copyright, 1893, by Wm. J. Kirkpatrick.

Follow All the Way.—CONCLUDED.

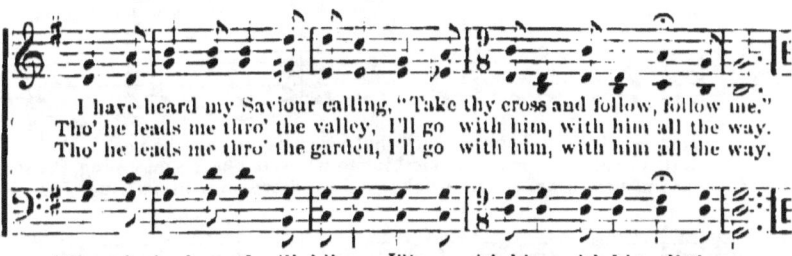

I have heard my Saviour calling, "Take thy cross and follow, follow me."
Tho' he leads me thro' the valley, I'll go with him, with him all the way.
Tho' he leads me thro' the garden, I'll go with him, with him all the way.

Where he leads me I will follow, I'll go with him, with him all the way.

4 ‖: Tho' the path be dark and dreary, :‖
I'll go with him, with him all the way.
5 ‖: Tho' he leads me to the conflict, :‖
I'll go with him, with him all the way.
6 ‖: Tho' he leads through fiery trials, :‖
I'll go with him, with him all the way.

7 ‖: I will follow on to know him, :‖
He's my Saviour, Saviour, Brother, Friend.
8 ‖: He will give me grace and glory, :‖
He will keep me, keep me all the way.
9 ‖: O 'tis sweet to follow Jesus, :‖
And be with him, with him all the way.

216 The Golden Key.

"Prayer is the key to unlock the door, and the bolt to shut in the night."

JNO. R. SWENEY.

1. Prayer is the key For the bending knee To open the morn's first hours;
2. Not a soul so sad, Nor a heart so glad, When cometh the shades of night,
3. Take the golden key In your hand and see, As the night tide drifts away,

See the incense rise To the starry skies, Like perfume from the flow'rs.
But the daybreak song Will the joy prolong, And some darkness turn to light.
How its blessed hold Is a crown of gold, Thro' the weary hours of day.

Copyright, 1875, by John J. Hood.

4 When the shadows fall,
And the vesper call
Is sobbing its low refrain,
'Tis a garland sweet
To the toil-dent feet,
And an antidote for pain.

5 Soon the year's dark door
Shall be shut no more;
Life's tears shall be wiped away,
As the pearl gates swing,
And the gold harps ring,
And the sun unsheathes for aye.

217. The Palace o' the King.

WILLIAM MITCHELL.   Mrs. Rev. J. G. WILSON.

1. It's a bonnie, bonnie warl' that we're liv-in' in the noo' An'
But in vain we look for something to which oor hearts may cling, For its
D. C.—For tho' bonnie are the snawflakes, an' the down on winter's wing, It's

sunny is the lan' that noo we aften traiv'll throo;
beauty is as naething . . . . to the palace o' the King.
fine to ken it daurna . . . . touch the palace o' the King.

We like the gild-ed simmer, wi' its mer-ry, mer-ry tread,
We sigh when hoar-y win-ter lays its beauties wi' the dead;

Copyright, 1893, by Jno. R. Sweney.

2 Then again, I've just been thinkin' that when a' thing here's sae bricht,
The sun in a' its grandeur, an' the mune wi' quiverin' licht,
The ocean i' the simmer; or the woodland i' the spring,
What maun it be up yonder, in the palace o' the King.
It's here we hae oor trials, an' its here that he prepares
His chosen for the raiment which the ransomed sinner wears.
An' it's here that he wad hear us 'mid oor tribulations sing.
"We'll trust oor God wha' reigneth in the palace o' the King."

The Palace o' the King.—CONCLUDED.

3 O its honor heaped on honor that his courtiers should be ta'en
Frae the waud'rin anes he died for in this warl' o' sin and pain,
An' its fu'est love an' service that the Christian aye should bring
To the feet o' him wha reigneth in the palace o' the King.
The time for sawin' seed, it is wearin, wearin dune;
An' the time for winnin' souls will be ower very sune.
Then let us a' be active, if a fruitfu' sheaf we'd bring
To adorn the royal table in the palace o' the King.

4 Nae nicht shall be in heaven, and nae desolatin' sea,
And nae tyrant hoofs shall trample in the city o' the free;
There's an everlastin' daylight, and a never fadin' spring,
Where the Lamb is a' the glory in the palace o' the King.
We see oor friends await us ower yonner at his gate;
Then let us a' be ready, for ye ken its gettin' late;
Let oor lamps be brichtly burnin'; let us raise oor voice and sing,
For sune we'll meet, to pairt nae mair, in the palace o' the King.

218 The Heaven-bound Mariner.

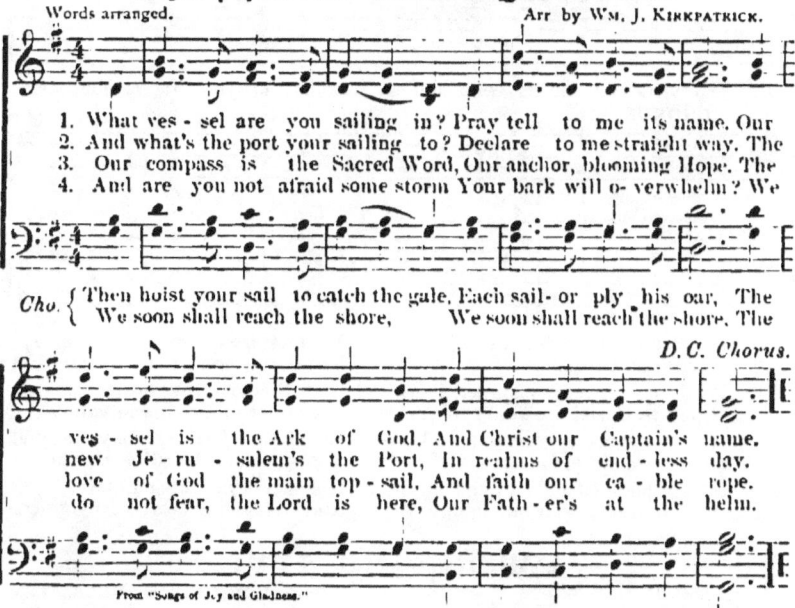

5 Heave out your boat, I too will go,
   If you can find me room.
 There's room for you, and all who will,
   Make no delay to come.   [storm

6 We've looked astern, through many a
   The Lord has brought us through;
 We're looking now ahead, and lo!
   The land appears in view.

7 The sun is up, the clouds are gone,
   The heavens above are clear,
 A city bright appears in sight,
   We soon shall round the pier.

8 And when we all are landed safe,
   On that celestial plain,
 Our song shall be "Worthy the Lamb
   That was for sinners slain."

Praise in Song—O

219. The Gospel Feast.

CHARLES WESLEY.
Cho. by H. L. G.
"Come, for all things are ready."
Luke xiv; 16.
H. L. GILMOUR. By per.

1. Come, sinners, to the gos-pel feast; It is for you, it is for me;
   Let ev-'ry soul be Je-sus' guest; It is for you, it is for me.
2. Ye need not one be left behind, It is for you, it is for me;
   For God hath bidden all mankind, It is for you, it is for me.

D.S.—O wea-ry wand'rer, come and see, It is for you, it is for me.

CHORUS.
Sal-vation full, sal-vation free, The price was paid on Cal-va-ry;

Copyright, 1899, by H. L. Gilmour.

3 Sent by my Lord, on you I call;
  The invitation is to all:
4 Come, all the world! come, sinner, thou!
  All things in Christ are ready now.
5 Come, all ye souls by sin oppressed,
  Ye restless wanderers after rest;
6 Ye poor, and maimed, and halt, and blind
  In Christ a hearty welcome find.

7 My message as from God receive;
  Ye all may come to Christ and live:
8 O let this love your hearts constrain,
  Nor suffer him to die in vain.
9 See him set forth before your eyes,
  That precious, bleeding sacrifice:
10 His offered benefits embrace,
   And freely now be saved by grace.

220. Awake, My Soul.

MEDLEY.
Tune, LOVING-KINDNESS. L. M.

1. Awake, my soul to joyful lays, And sing thy great Redeemer's praise;
2. He saw me ru-ined in the fall, Yet loved me not-withstanding all;

Awake, My Soul.—CONCLUDED.

He just-ly claims a song from me, His lov-ing-kind-ness, oh, how free!
He saved me from my lost e-state, His lov-ing-kind-ness, oh, how great!

Lov-ing-kindness, lov-ing-kindness, His lov-ing-kind-ness, oh, how free!
Lov-ing-kindness, lov-ing-kindness, His lov-ing-kind-ness, oh, how great!

3 Though num'rous hosts of mighty foes,
Though earth and hell my way oppose,
He safely leads my soul along,
His loving-kindness, oh, how strong!

4 When trouble, like a gloomy cloud,
Has gathered thick, and thundered loud,
He near my soul has always stood,
His loving-kindness, oh, how good!

221 My Faith Looks Up to Thee.

RAY PALMER.   L. MASON.

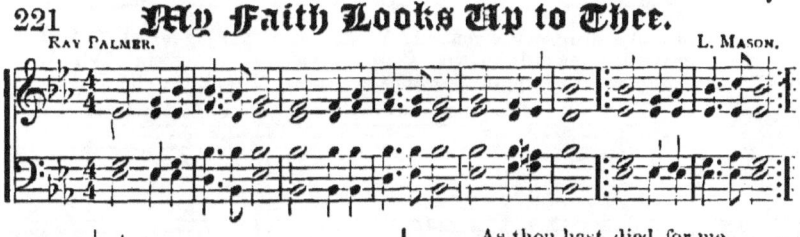

1 My faith looks up to thee,
Thou Lamb of Calvary,
Saviour divine!
Now hear me while I pray;
Take all my guilt away;
Oh, let me from this day
Be wholly thine!

2 May thy rich grace impart
Strength to my fainting heart,
My zeal inspire!

As thou hast died for me,
Oh, may my love to thee
Pure, warm, and changeless be—
A living fire!

3 While life's dark maze I tread,
And griefs around me spread,
Be thou my guide;
Bid darkness turn to day,
Wipe sorrow's tears away,
Nor let me ever stray
From thee aside.

4 When ends life's transient dream,
When death's cold sullen stream
Shall o'er me roll,
Blest Saviour! then, in love,
Fear and distrust remove;
Oh, bear me safe above—
A ransomed soul!

Tell it Out with Gladness.—CONCLUDED.

feel. Tell it out, tell it out with glad-ness.
world the joy you feel,

223. Lord, I'm Coming Home.

W. J. K.
With great feeling.
WM. J. KIRKPATRICK.

1. I've wandered far a-way from God, Now I'm coming home;
2. I've wast-ed ma-ny pre-cious years, Now I'm coming home;
3. I'm tired of sin and stray-ing, Lord, Now I'm coming home;
4. My soul is sick, my heart is sore, Now I'm coming home;

The paths of sin too long I've trod, Lord, I'm coming home.
I now re-pent with bit-ter tears, Lord, I'm coming home.
I'll trust thy love, be-lieve thy word, Lord, I'm coming home.
My strength renew, my hope re-store, Lord, I'm coming home.

D.S.—O-pen wide thine arms of love, Lord, I'm coming home.

CHORUS.

Coming home, coming home, Nev-er more to roam;

Copyright, 1892, by Wm. J. Kirkpatrick.

5 My only hope, my only plea,
   Now I'm coming home,
   That Jesus died, and died for me,
   Lord, I'm coming home.

6 I need his cleansing blood I know,
   Now I'm coming home;
   Oh, wash me whiter than the snow,
   Lord, I'm coming home.

Brother, Come.—CONCLUDED.

Say-ing ten-der-ly. Come, come, come un-to me, Come un-to
Saves them will-ing-ly.
Turn not scorn-ful-ly.
Un-re-sist-ing-ly.

me and rest; Come, come, come unto me, Come unto me and rest.

230. Jesus will Meet You There.

W. L. K.
W. Lewis Kane.

1. Come to Calv'ry's mount to-day, Je-sus will meet you there;
   Look and live without de-lay, Je-sus will meet you there.

CHORUS.

Come to Jesus, Don't stay away, my friend; Come to Jesus, Dont stay away.

Copyright, 1888, by Jno. R. Sweney.

2 Rest beneath the hallowed cross,
  Jesus will meet you there;
  Saving mercy gained for loss,
  Jesus will meet you there.

3 Come and join his faithful band,
  Jesus will meet you there;
  Take his mighty, helping hand,
  Jesus will meet you there,

4 At the blessed mercy seat,
  Jesus will meet you there;
  Come with this assurance sweet,
  Jesus will meet you there.

5 You'll find rest in heaven at last,
  Jesus will meet you there;
  And be happy with the blest,
  Jesus will meet you there.

TOPICAL INDEX.

ACCEPTANCE. 63.
ADVENT, 36.
ASPIRATION, 75, 224.
ATONEMENT, 71, 74, 79.
AWAKENING, 63, 177, 184, 185.
BIBLE, 183.
CHRISTIAN ACTIVITY, 24, 29, 44, 50, 51, 65, 113, 114, 131, 139, 155, 169, 170, 212.
CONFIDENCE, 25, 35, 77, 80, 81, 87, 94, 111, 150, 203, 226, 223.
CONSECRATION, 7, 90, 91, 105, 169, 200.
CONSOLATION, 109, 134.
DEVOTION, 15, 61, 75, 101, 104, 112, 120, 126, 151, 160, 163, 193, 196, 209, 210, 211, 215, 221.
ENCOURAGEMENT, 88, 116, 142, 156, 186, 208.
FAITH, 41, 221.
FELLOWSHIP, 99.
FORGIVENESS, 144, 145.
GOSPEL, 94, 138.
GRACE, 129.
GUIDANCE, 13, 117, 174, 187.
HEAVEN, 11, 12, 58, 62, 67, 72, 92, 93, 97, 102, 103, 134, 171, 180, 194, 215, 217.
INVITATION, 9, 18, 23, 31, 34, 36, 57, 62, 70, 74, 89, 95, 108, 119, 136, 137, 147, 148, 149, 152, 167, 175, 190, 198, 202, 219, 229.

JESUS, 1, 8, 19, 26, 28, 32, 36, 39, 45, 68, 70, 84, 91, 163, 168, 188, 205, 231.
LIVING, 60, 127, 132, 195.
MISSIONARY, 37, 83, 204.
OPENING, 33, 211, 213.
PENITENCE, 46, 98, 115, 130, 197, 223.
PERSEVERANCE, 47.
PRAISE, 4, 14, 64, 78, 86, 87, 135, 140, 143, 161, 199, 201, 206, 207, 213.
PRAYER, 55, 122, 216.
PROMISES, 5, 73.
PROVIDENCE, 16, 17, 40, 73, 128, 228.
PURITY, 125, 144, 224.
REFUGE, 8, 48, 121, 159.
REJOICING, 21, 22, 27, 42, 43, 53, 178, 225.
RESIGNATION, 203.
REST, 19, 96, 107, 176.
RESURRECTION, 106.
REWARD, 30.
SABBATH SCHOOL, 100, 118, 178.
SALVATION, 10, 38, 54, 59, 68, 74, 124, 141, 146, 154, 162, 173, 182, 191, 192.
SANCTIFICATION, 69, 153.
SUPPLICATION, 110, 166, 205, 209.
TESTIMONY, 49, 61, 66, 69, 82, 85, 123, 146, 157, 158, 164, 172, 181, 189, 214, 222, 227.
TRIUMPH, 20, 76, 106, 133.
TRUSTING, 6, 52, 174.

INDEX.

Titles in CAPITALS; First lines in roman type.

Title/First line	HYMN	Title/First line	HYMN	Title/First line	HYMN
A FRIEND INDEED,	39	BOUNDLESS AND FR–	74	FLOW IN, MY GOD,	160
Again we come with.	33	BREAK FORTH IN S–	4	FOLLOW ALL THE W–	215
Again within the h–	25	BROTHER, COME,	229	FOR HE CARETH FOR	16
Ah, many years my b–	144	Brother, the Saviour	229	From my sin and dan–	163
A joyful song I love–	86	BUILDING DAY BY DAY	60	From that dear cross	162
Alas! and did my S–	173	By the cross we con–	133	From the stranger c–	72
A LITTLE TALK,	122	BY THIS WE CONQUER	133		
All along life's rug–	6			Give praise to God,	64
ALL OUR NEED SUP–	73	CALLING THEE TO–	89	Give the very best to	15
Alone with thee, my–	90	CALVARY'S STREAM	162	GIVE THY LIFE TO JE–	113
ALWAYS SOMETHING–	32	CHOOSE THE SAVIOUR	202	GLAD TIDINGS OF JOY	54
Amid the trials which	228	Choose you this day,	136	GLORY, HE SAVES,	227
AN OFFERING OF PR–	14	CHRIST, OUR PASSO–	192	Glory to Jesus, he s–	227
ANYTHING, LORD, FOR	7	Christ the Lord is c–	36	Go as an humble dis–	155
ANYWHERE IN HEAV–	180	COME AND BUY,	56	GOD GIVETH HIS BEST	128
Are you growing h–	88	COME AND NO LONG–	190	God is my salvation,	150
Are you happy in the	222	Come home, come h–	57	GOOD NEWS,	38
As Jacob, when wea–	154	Come, sinners, to the	219	Go tell to the nations	37
ASTRAY,	114	Come to Calvary's m–	230		
A SUNNY SIDE OF L–	156	Come to Jesus, bring	167	HALLELUJAH'S WE'LL	78
At last, my King and	130	Come to Jesus, wand–	202	HAPPY DAYS,	43
A trembling soul, I s–	71	Come, weary traveler	89	HAPPY REST WILL J–	107
At the beautiful gate	68	Come while the Sav–	190	Hark! from the joy–	96
AT THY FEET,	130	COME, WHOSOEVER W–	57	Have you learned to,	149
Awake, my soul, to	220	Come, ye saints of the	78	Have you, my dear b–	123
		CONSOLATION,	109	Have you nothing to–	51
Beautiful star of pr–	5	*Creation, L. M. D.*	206	HEAVENLY MANNA,	129
Behold me standing–	70			HEAVENLY MUSIC,	58
BETTER DAYS,	142	Dear Jesus, canst thou	98	HE HEALETH ALL MY	189
BID HIM WELCOME,	34	DO NOT MAKE LIGHT	137	HE IS MY REFUGE,	8
BLESSED FRIEND,	94	Do what you can for	212	HE'LL MENTION TH–	145
BLESSED HIDING,	19	Do you seek the gold–	108	Here, while we gath–	211
BLESSED JESUS, I AM	126	Draw me near to thee	101	HE TOOK MY PLACE,	71
Blessed Lord, I am w–	46			I always go to Jesus,	8
Blessed refuge of the	159	Earthly sweets will	32	I AM COMING, BLESSED	46
Blessed words of tru–	183	Everything in Jesus,	91	I AM SAVED, PRAISE,	66
Bless the hour when–	53	Eye hath not seen	102	I am walking to-day,	66
BLESS THE LORD, MY	199			I am walking to-day,	146
BLIND BARTIMEUS,	172	FAITHFUL AND TRUE	87	I am walking with my	120
Boast thou not of thy	35	Father of all, whose	207		

INDEX.

I am with you, oh, . 13	Keep me close to . 151	On the heights, . 153
I ask, O Lord, that . 41		On the other side, 134
I cannot drift beyond 117	Lay up thy treas-. . 35	On the way, . . 214
If ye love me, saith . 110	Leaning on the ev- 226	On to victory shall . 20
I glory in the cross of 164	Let my gaze be fixed, 1	Onward, rejoicing m. 178
I have heard my Sav- 215	Let us go and possess 191	Open the door for 115
I have left the land of 69	Light is shining j. . 88	O praise the Lord, 161
I heard a sweet voice 82	Like a shepherd, ten- 187	O, the winds were h. 176
I hope to live th. . 11	Live unto him, . 127	Our Lamb is slain, . 192
I know 'tis the voice. 111	Living in Canaan, . 191	Our loving Friend 193
I lift the flood-gate of 160	Living like Christ 195	Out in the breakers . 170
I'll praise my Re-. 143	Living to save the lost 195	Out of darkness into . 10
I'll sing my dear Re- 27	Long ago, at the even- 124	O wandering one, . 18
I love thee, I love thee 196	Lord, I'm coming h. 223	
I'm dwelling in the 69		Prayer is the key, . 216
I'm free, . . . 25	Marching in the L. 178	Precious lessons, . 100
I'm happy, I'm happy 143	More about Jesus w. 231	Precious Saviour, k. . 151
In all my thoughts, in 112	My body, mind, and . 200	Precious the mes- . 186
In all thy ways ac- . 174	My consecration, . 200	
I now believe, . 173	My faith looks up to . 221	Redeeming grace, . 22
In the city, . . 108	My Father's care, . 40	Remembered bless- 85
In the day of trial, in 39	My heart has been . 166	Rest awhile, . . 107
In the glory land, 103	My only interces- . 157	Resting 'neath his 158
In the Lord is our h. 201	My Saviour has pur- . 188	Rest, sweet rest, . 96
In the presence of 30	My Saviour, when . 26	Rise, O my soul, to . 127
In the shadow of thy 19	My soul sings glory . 145	Rouse, ye christian . 139
In the ways of the L. 49		
Invocation, . . 33	No fault in Jesus,. 26	Salvation ! O the joy- 141
I once was a stranger 61	Nothing to fear, . 52	Save one, . . 170
I once was blind, but 189	Nothing to pay. for a- 79	Saviour, hear my p. . 209
I sang, one day, a sad 85	Not one forgotten 17	Saviour, how I need . 210
I shall be whiter. 166		Saviour, take me . 209
I take my portion fr. 203	O come, O come ! for 148	Saviour, to thee, . 211
It's a bonnie, bonnie 217	O for a heart that is . 224	See I a sail amid the. 50
I've wandered far a- . 223	Oft hast thou heard a 185	Simple faith in Jesus, 73
I was a wayward, w. 181	Oft I seem to hear . 58	Singing all the w. 21
I will praise him, . 165	Oh, bless the Lord, m. 199	Singing and trusting, 52
I will sing you a song 95	Oh, bless the Lord, w. 214	Sing on the way to Zi- 42
I would be thine, . 112	Oh, come to the f. . 18	Sing praise to God, . 135
	Oh, for a vision of Je- 104	Sing with me in joy- . 165
Jehovah, my Sav- . 61	Oh, glad are our h. . 87	Some blessed day, . 92
Jehovah's sover- . 207	Oh, he's a wonder- 188	Someday, but when, I 92
Jesus, come in to-day 75	Oh, Master, save, . 124	Star of promise, . 5
Jesus in Galilee, . 108	Oh, my hope is as b. . 11	Steadfast faith, . 41
Jesus is my helper, . 28	Oh, sigh not in sor- . 156	Step out on the p. . 198
Jesus leads, . . 187	Oh, such wonder- . 45	Still out of Christ, . 152
Jesus lives, and lo. 163	Oh, 'tis sweet to live. 105	Stop, sinner, stop, you 184
Jesus, lover of my . 205	Oh, what a wonderful 54	Sunshine in the s. . 225
Jesus, my hope, my . 115	Oh, what wilt thou do 177	Sweet land of rest, . 171
Jesus my Saviour did 45	Oh, yes, I'm re- . 82	Sweetly now are an- . 103
Jesus now is stand- 34	O mourner in Zion, . 198	Sweet wordso'or-arch 22
Jesus only, . . 105	On Calvary's cross, . 74	
Jesus, the light, . 1	One by one the sheav. 30	Take me, Saviour, . 126
Jesus will meet y. 230	One day nearer, . 97	Tell it out with o. 222
Just as I am, without 197	On Jordan's stormy . 194	Tell the glad sto- . 128
	Only a little word, . 44	Tell the glad tid- 83
Keep close to Je- . 179	Only to follow, day . 43	Tell to the nations 87

Tell to the nations the	83	The Saviour found	181	We'll surely con-.	76
Thank God and take	47	The song-land,	116	We love to gather at.	55
That old, old story	94	The spacious firma-	206	What a comfort to	80
The beautiful har-	12	The stairway of l.	49	What a fellowship,	226
The blessed song,	149	The sweet Beulah	146	Whate'er it be,	203
The cross is my an-	81	The winds were h.	176	What vessel are you	218
The door stands o-.	23	The wonderful s. .	84	What wilt thou do	177
The earth is the L. .	4	They will come to us	134	What wouldst thou .	7
The evening sun is s.	97	Tho' dark the night .	122	Whence Jesus came .	172
The everlasting s.	140	Thou art my refuge,.	121	When Christ, the Son	106
The foes of life we	77	Thou art with me, S.	99	When faints the h. .	107
The fold was warm, .	114	Tho' numbered w. the	157	When my warfare is.	180
The fountain now.	59	Tho' the pathway s. .	142	When our shattered .	116
The golden key,	216	Thou thinkest, L. .	228	When out from E-	129
The good ship Zion	148	Tho' waves dash a- .	81	When the port of h. .	140
The gospel feast, .	219	Thronging about him	168	When we all get h. .	208
The heaven-bound, .	218	Throw out the life-l. .	29	When you start for .	179
The heaven's de-	206	'Tis thy own voice in	109	Where, but to thee	48
The joyful sound, .	141	To be forever thi.	90	Where is thy soul?	185
The ladder of mer-	154	To the rescue, .	50	Where is thy sting	106
The light that n. .	132	Traveler, turn, O turn	119	Where shall I go, my	48
The Lord dwell-	77	Trusting, . .	6	While as Christians .	16
The Master com-	137			While saints and an-.	161
The palace o' the .	217	Upon the King's h. .	21	While we pray, and .	9
There are heights	76	Up with the morn-	24	White as snow,	144
There are songs, glad	67	Use me, O my gra-	169	Who will follow Je-.	147
There is a bond of u.	193			Why are you lan-	56
There is a fountain .	59	Waiting for you, .	31	Why not now? .	9
There is a joy that .	22	Wash me, O Lamb of	125	Why not to-day? .	175
There is a light that.	132	Watchman, tell us of	204	Why will you roam .	31
There's a life on the .	153	We are building in .	60	Will you be among .	63
There's a lovely har-.	12	We are singing on .	93	Will you meet me in	62
There's a wonderful .	94	Weary and sin-sick .	84	Winning souls for	139
There's a word of ten-	17	Weary in spirit, w. .	186	Within thy courts, O	213
There's no comfort in	158	We come in his name	118	Wonderful story of l.	182
There's not a bird .	40	We come to thee, O.	14	Wonderful tidings b.	38
There's power in the	138	We know it is true .	128	Words of truth .	183
There's sunshine in .	225	We live to serve the .	131	Working for Jesus, .	65

224

www.ingramcontent.com/pod-product-compliance
Lightning Source LLC
Chambersburg PA
CBHW021843230426
43669CB00008B/1064